The Weapon: A Guide to Self-Love and Escaping the Toxic Cycle

C. C. Griffiths

Second Edition September 2020

ISBN 9798655703513
Binding type: Paperback

Book Cover © 2020 Aaron-lee Griffiths

Instagram @Theweapon20

CONTENTS

Introduction

Firstly, despite what you may have assumed this book is not here to convince you all men are trash. We're not going to spend the next X amount of pages man-bashing and blaming men for all of society's problems. Players, cheaters, fuckboys etc... The list of derogatory names for men is growing continuously. However, for some reason, women are still flocking to men with less than desirable attributes. Shamefully, it's time some of us women realise it's not them that need to change - it's us.

Controversial opinion, I know but when our relationships go wrong rarely do we ask ourselves what part we had to play in how things turned out. We also don't look into the reasons why we have chosen to be with people that are bad for us. Without this much-needed self-reflection, we can find ourselves being heartbroken repeatedly. We walk into the same type of relationships, again and again, expecting different results.

We often love others more than we love ourselves putting their needs above ours hoping it will change things. We undervalue ourselves and neglect to love ourselves. Self-love is often underestimated, perhaps even misunderstood. It's important because it affects how we view ourselves. It can take years to fully learn to accept and love who we are. Many different things can have a negative influence on how we see ourselves. We draw a lot from how we believe others see us. Often letting somebody else's ability to see our value, depreciate our self-worth.

The unhealthy relationships we find ourselves in may not even seem enjoyable to us but for some reason, we keep entering/staying in them. This is all down to a lack of self-love. Without realising it there's something we get out of experiencing this type of hurt over and over again. There's something within us that is being stimulated by these relationships. Whatever it is gives us a reason to stay in a relationship longer than we should. Some of us endure being in toxic relationships because we equate this intense passion to love. Many cling onto the potential of feeling the love from others that they don't know how to give to themselves. The reason many of us do this is that the love we feel for ourselves is low. We often love others more than we love ourselves.

For people that have been in a string of bad relationships, the trauma is likely to have had a negative impact on the way they see themselves and their ability to feel worthy of love. It may not have been multiple relationships that made them think negatively about themselves, but one significant one. Either way, it's important to rebuild the parts of ourselves that we feel have been damaged.

Relationships have a huge influence on our mental state of mind. They can make us happy, depressed, more confident or insecure. Within our relationships, there are so many feelings and emotions that we go through. All of these feelings end up affecting how we feel about ourselves overall. This can negatively impact how we see ourselves. Damaging our self-esteem and making us doubt our worth.

The danger of our self-esteem being damaged is that it impacts how much love we have for ourselves. We stop looking out for ourselves. Decisions become based on making others happy instead of us. We need to identify why we chose to be in a hurtful relationship that lowered our self-esteem. Without knowing this, it's harder for us to avoid choosing a relationship like this again.

Unknowingly we will be likely to jump back into relationships with another person that makes us question our value. Constantly chipping away at our own self-esteem by doing so. What we don't realise is when we do this we become weaker. The weaker we are the more susceptible we become to surrounding ourselves with people that take advantage of us.

If you leave your front door unlocked and get burgled, you learn to lock the door next time. The same safety precautions should be given to your mental state too. You have to know where your weaknesses are to protect yourself.

The Weapon will give you the tools you need to build your self-esteem and love yourself again. Ultimately, making you a more confident version of yourself. Turning you into somebody that values your time and energy and is aware of the choices that they're making. Without realising it, a lot of us have fallen out of the habit of taking care of ourselves. No more ending up with guys that aren't serious about you.

The Weapon is mainly for women that have had enough of bad toxic relationships. Women that want to go on a journey to learn to love themselves the way they should be loved. By acknowledging that we've had a part to play in how our relationships have turned out. We allow ourselves the opportunity to take back power over our own lives.

In this life, we have to be accountable for the things we do. Which means understanding why we chose men that are no good for us and why we stay with them. While reading this book you'll be challenged to ask yourself why you stayed in situations that hurt you. It's then up to you to use your answers to create a better you. A version of you that loves and cares about yourself.

For you to get the most out of reading *The Weapon* ask yourself what your purpose is for reading it. The best thing to do is set an intention for what you want to get out of reading this. Once you've decided on your intention, write it down. Remembering your intention will keep you focused especially during the parts you may find hard to read. You'll also have to be willing to change your mentality and to do that, you need to be ready to hear messages that may feel harsh.

Know whether you want to gain healing from a previous relationship or understanding. Alternatively, you may just want to rebuild your self-esteem after a string of bad relationships. Whatever it is, *The Weapon* will help you learn and grow so you don't make these mistakes again. There'll be various exercises you'll be asked to do throughout the book so always have a pen and paper at the ready.

Learning to love yourself is a journey. Sometimes the best time to start that journey is after a difficult relationship, as this is usually when we feel at our lowest and most emotionally vulnerable.

Throughout this book, we will cover multiple scenarios that you may relate to and might have contributed to you losing part of your self-esteem. You will begin to take steps to gain clarity over the past and start to love yourself again. Along the way learning how to increase the value you place on yourself. One of the best things about this kind of therapy is the selfishness you get to experience. It's all about you. You get to understand why you are the way you are. How tiny experiences in your life have had a bigger impact than you realised.

There are four main sections in this book with key things we will be covering. All equally as important as each other.

1. **Let Go Of The Past**
   Learn how to recover from the trauma of your past relationships. This section is perfect for anyone trying to get over someone

2. **Know Who You Are**
   Understand what has made you attracted to people that are no good, so you can steer clear of them in future

3. **Weaponise Your Self-love**
   A must-read section to teach you about truly loving yourself

4. **Know Your Position**

This section delves into different types of unhealthy relationships. Learn how not to compromise on the type of relationship you want

Read the sections that you feel are most relevant to you. Each part will help you adjust the current way you think when it comes to yourself and relationships. Doing the exercises laid out will help you realise additional things about yourself. The more you write during these exercises, the more you will have to hold yourself accountable. Doing the work proves your commitment to making a change. You will always be able to refer back to what you have written in your notebook in the future.

Take these exercises as seriously as you can as this is where most of the learning comes from. If you were in school you wouldn't just listen to the teacher you would make notes and do the exercises required, so that you learn effectively. There is power in the pen so when you think about things and write them down you're taking the time to let it resonate with you. It's too easy to read books like this and agree with all the points made, then revert straight back to your old ways. True growth has to come from you. You have to be ready and willing to change.

In order to change you need to make a promise to yourself that you're going to do all of the exercises in this book. Sticking to this promise shows the level of commitment you have to yourself. Each of the exercises are there to teach you a lesson that will benefit you so don't just read past it.

Discovering Accountability

One of the biggest lessons you are about to learn is accountability. Whilst trying to get over painful relationships it's easy to place blame on the other person. Rarely do we look at ourselves and assess what it is that we did wrong. Especially when in our mind our ex was horrible to us and we didn't deserve to be treated that way.

Nobody wants to admit that in the movie of their lives they were the villain. That they played a role in how badly their ex treated them. This is why accountability is so important. Many of us choose to stay in relationships that are hurtful to us. We have the power to leave but instead of leaving, we stayed and wallowed in sadness. We stay knowing the pain that we're in. At some stage, we have to look at ourselves and ask why?

Many of us have been in toxic relationships but haven't wanted to acknowledge how toxic the relationship is. We may be surrounded by friends and family that are also in toxic relationships so it all seems very normal to us. We have to understand that being in a toxic relationship is a choice. There are many people that choose healthy and stable relationships. If that's not you, then you should know what the reason is for that.

Some of us love the drama and the attention that comes with being in a relationship that's no good for us. Feeling sorry for ourselves for having to endure misery. Breaking news is… it's not a relationship we **had** to endure, we **chose** to be there. Being in a toxic relationship is like going to a dominatrix that straps you into a chair and beats you. Despite you having a safe word to make them stop at any time. You decide to stay strapped to the chair and take the beatings. You then make every excuse under the sun, as to why you should stay seated in that chair getting beaten. For many of us, once we finally decide to leave, we ask our dominatrix why they kept beating us. They would answer us and say it's because we never left the chair.

We expect the dominatrix to apologise to us for beating us and take no accountability for the fact we stayed in the chair for so long or that we decided to sit in the chair in the first place. Sometimes we even volunteer to sit back in the chair again.

In this scenario, the dominatrix has nothing to apologise for. They treated you the way you allowed them to, and when you didn't leave, they continued to treat you in that way. They do not owe you an apology for that. You owe yourself the apology for sitting in the chair in the first place. In relationships, we endure a lot of mistreatment from our partner but decide to stay. The only conclusion that can be drawn from you staying is that on some level you enjoyed it.

It's hard to accept because on a human level we believe our dominatrix should have seen we were in pain and stopped beating us, but in this world, you have to be responsible for yourself. We can't expect others to show us the love that we don't show ourselves. By continuing to stay strapped into a chair that causes you pain you're not practising self-love. You're making the choice to let somebody emotionally beat you continuously.

Putting yourself in this position is one of the most hateful things you could do to yourself. Controversial fact, but it's us that control our own lives. Simply because men can only do to you, what you allow them to. A lack of self-love will have you tolerating far more than you should.

It's time to feel empowered by knowing you have the ability to create your own happiness. Along with knowing this, realise you have the power to create our own misfortune too. Then make a decision to start choosing things that benefit you and don't harm you.

Self-worth, Self-esteem and Self-love

People often think if they rate themselves highly on looks or achievements that means they love themselves. Self-love is actually much more complicated than that. You can believe that you're amazing and deserve the world but if you don't treat yourself in that way, it's very unlikely you love yourself as much as you think you do.

The love we have for ourselves is tied into our esteem. Our self-esteem is symptomatic of how good we feel about ourselves. Other words for esteem are respect, adore and appreciate. These adjectives describe the way we need to begin to view ourselves. At times our insecurities get in the way of this and play a big part in how we feel about ourselves. Your insecurities create victims out of the parts of yourself you don't feel good about. The more control you allow your insecurities to have, the lower your self-esteem will be.

People often attribute insecurities to their physical appearance but actually, your insecurities can be broader than that. Insecurities are the judgements that you make about yourself. They can be about anything and are usually based on the things you hate the most about yourself. You could be someone that doesn't have a lot of friends and this can manifest within you as one of your insecurities. Having you believe that nobody ever wants to be your friend and if anybody else brings it up the subject you feel attacked.

Alternatively, you may just hate the size of your forehead. Either way, part of building your self-esteem is learning to love yourself including your flaws. Accepting the things about yourself that you hate as part of you, and learning how to live with them. Switch your focus to more positive things about yourself. Too many of us pay more attention to the negative voice in our head, over the positive one. This is something we will unpack more in the weaponise your self-love section.

Self-love is an important weapon. It changes the way we think about ourselves and others. The love we have for ourselves sets the standard for us. It influences how we want to be treated and massively contributes to our insecurities. Our insecurities can make us see and expect the worst from others.

If you have ever fallen out with someone you care about you may have noticed that they assumed you think about them in a way that you don't. Believing things that you've never said i.e "she thinks I'm a slut" "she thinks she's better than me". Secretly these would have been statements the person thinks about themselves that they worry others secretly think too.

A secure person never worries about people thinking these things about them. Whereas insecure people project their thoughts about themselves onto others.

A lot of the time we judge others by our own standards. This projection can be both positive and negative. At times it can make us think the best of people because we wouldn't act in a certain way we don't expect others to either. On the flip side because we would behave in a certain way we may fear others would also. It all depends on the kind of person you are. The spiteful things we worry others would do to us are a reflection of the way our own mind works and not theirs. Things we worry others will think of us are actually things we think about ourselves. In this way, insecurities can have a lot of power over us. Influencing how we act and how we let things affect us.

To increase your self-esteem you need to build on the things you like and learn to show yourself respect. You may not necessarily feel like you're an insecure person. However, the lack of love and respect you show to yourself will prove how much self-esteem you have.

Many people rely on others to help them build their self-esteem. If others give them the attention they need they feel validated in some way. Relying on others for validation can become problematic as the value you place on yourself comes from other people rather than from you. This is where your self-worth crosses over with your self-esteem. Your personal sense of self-worth reflects how much self-esteem you have.

Let Go of the Past

Seeking Closure

I could just simply tell you closure doesn't exist but it's not as easy as that. You truly have to understand that for yourself. If you've ever gotten over someone before you probably accepted it didn't exist then. You may have even believed closure didn't exist until you felt like you needed again. Accepting it's over when you still love the person is hard. You're only human so these feelings are understandable. This is something we all struggle with but true closure can only come from within.

The need for closure is that feeling of unrest when our brain can't make sense of what has happened. We truly believe that with one conversation all of our unanswered questions will not only be finally answered but that the answers will make complete sense. No longer leaving us wondering where it went wrong. Then we will be able to accept the break-up and move on.

During a breakup, you have to be able, to be honest with yourself. Self-honesty plays an important part in learning to love ourselves fully. It's in your best interest to understand how you feel so you can make decisions that are right for you.

When you embark on your quest for closure and set out to have that conversation about what went wrong, you need to truly understand what your objective is. Know if your main objective is to reach a resolution and heal your wound, or to make them feel bad about what they did to you?

Some people in the search for closure, seek vengeance rather than conversation. Believing that hurting their ex in any way will relieve them from their pain. Sadly, all vengeance does is continue to give away your precious energy to a situation that doesn't serve you. You may feel angry and want to lash out but this will just make the situation toxic.

The feelings of anger will pass eventually. When it does you will still have feelings of hurt and there's no avoiding that, unfortunately. When you're hurt you just want to feel whole again. We believe that closure gives us that feeling. The thing that you need to know about closure is that it's something only you can give yourself. You could have 20 conversations with your ex for closure and still never get any actual closure from it. You could try writing down every question you have, they could answer them all and you would still feel like you need closure.

In life sometimes you have to learn to accept the apologies that you never received. Sometimes actual apologies you do receive, may not be genuine anyway. When your ex apologises/apologised to you, would you be able to adequately assess whether or not the apology was genuine? We would hope that it's genuine but it could also come from any of the below...

- True remorse and acceptance of their wrong behaviour
- Them trying to move past the awkwardness of the conversation
- Them trying to make themselves feel better for being a bad person

No matter what the answer is, we hear whatever we want to hear. People generally don't like to admit that they're shit, horrible or inconsiderate human beings. Apologising is often the polite thing to do when you've hurt someone. It's really the very least a person can do to right their wrongs and redeem themselves as a decent human being. They may genuinely feel terrible, however, you are not obliged to forgive them just for the sake of their ego. You should forgive them for the sake of yours. The presence of an actual apology is not necessary for you to forgive. Don't put so much weight behind hearing an apology from them.

When you choose to forgive someone you're allowing that person to release themselves from the burden of guilt. The apology is their way of begging you to relieve them of that guilt. It serves them more than it does you. However, you should learn to accept their apology whether they've given you one or not.

Behind the intention of an apology is a plea for forgiveness. This is a mercy that the other person may not seem like they deserve. However, you deserve it. You deserve not to hold feelings of bitterness and resentment. You should forgive that person for the sake of your own healing. They don't even need to know you've forgiven them. If we break down the word 'forgive' it's all about you...

To Forgive
From the Oxford dictionary
1. stop feeling angry or resentful towards (someone) for an offence, flaw, or mistake

Anger and resentment are feelings **you** hold not them. These negative feelings keep you from moving forward and allow the person to take up space in your mind. When you're healing from a breakup you want to shift to a place of positivity and love. This shift will allow you to attract better things into your life. When you consciously choose to forgive someone you make the choice to no longer hold ill-feeling towards them.

You forgiving them will help you no longer hold any feelings towards them whatsoever. It's okay to forgive someone and still acknowledge that they caused you pain. Forgiving them doesn't mean they need to be back in your life either. It's simply an act of release that you have chosen to undertake. Giving away those negative feelings you have towards them.

Exercise

You might find it difficult to simply forgive a person that has hurt you so greatly. To make this easier let's reprogramme the way you see this relationship. Before we do that we need to understand how you feel about the relationship now.

This exercise is purely for you so remember nobody is judging you. Be honest about your feelings towards your ex.

Before you read on, grab a pen and paper and start by writing between 5-10 words or statements that you feel that describe your relationship overall.

If you read on before doing the exercise it might impact your results so start writing your statements now...

Now that you have written these look back at what you have written and ask yourself the following questions...

1. How many of the words you've written provoke a negative emotion?

2. Do these descriptions respect you as a person?

3. Does it respect your time?

4. Are these words/statements filled with anger?

5. Is there still hope for your relationship in any of these statements?

For you to have closure your statements/words should read like the below...

I am grateful for the lessons I learnt from the relationship

The relationship has made me the person I am today

I learnt a lot about myself from my relationship with this person

This person hurt me but I forgive them

I've let go of the resentment I have towards them

I'm glad it's over now

Freedom

I know I'm better off without them

I'm over it

The last statement is obviously the best one that we are all hoping we can honestly say one day. If you notice these statements are not bitter or resentful. They are not holding on to pieces of a relationship that are no longer there are no hopeful intentions of a reunion. Most importantly the statements show respect to you. On this journey of self-love and evaluating our self-worth it's very important you don't let ill-feelings about your previous relationship drag you down. You have never wasted your love. You are not unworthy and your ex hasn't taken any part of you that you can't get back.

When you love yourself, you respect your time and the journeys that have made you the person that you are today. It's easier to hate the person you have become if you hate the journeys you've been on. We have to find ways to turn our negative experiences into positive ones otherwise we will struggle to even like ourselves.

Statements such as 'wasted my time' only devalue your time. The statement 'It was fake and full of lies' shows the anger that you're still holding onto. Your statements should hold gratitude for yourself and the relationship. This is a more positive feeling that allows you to let go and be thankful that the relationship is over and grateful for the lessons you learned. You're now able to experience something better.

Exercise

Look back at your answers if you see that they are more negative than positive re-write the 10 statements but start each one with 'I am grateful that the relationship...' finish this sentence with your own words. For example...

"I am grateful that the relationship taught me what I no longer want to accept "

You owe it to yourself to honour the time you spent together and the feelings you had. Shifting your mind frame to one that puts the relationship in the past will help you gain the much-needed closure you are after. Without doing this you'll hold onto the relationship and your brain will continue to try and make sense of everything. You have to accept that you will never truly understand everything that went wrong, this fact has to be okay with you.

Understanding the Split

In all situations, there's a reason why you split up, or why this person is no longer in your life in the same way anymore. Whether it's down to destiny just playing itself out or because the situation became too toxic to endure anymore. The major thing for you to see here is that there were two sides to your love story and you only ever got to read your half of the book.

Imagine only reading every other page of a book, without the full story, how could you ever fully understand what kind of story the book was telling? When you are finally able to read the other pages and put the whole story together, you will find the story wasn't about what you thought. On your side, it was a love story, and you made decisions based on believing that's what it was.

During the relationship, there were many signs you chose to ignore so you could continue to tell yourself the story you wanted. Then after the breakup, you finally saw glimpses of the pages from their book and found out their story was different from yours. This can be a painful realisation. Especially when you know that if you had been honest with yourself at the time, the book should have been closed ages ago. Don't punish yourself over this. It's now time to move to a place of acceptance.

Right now, you know it's over and you can choose to end your story here. Continuing to look for closure is making the decision to keep the book open. Understand that going back to re-read the pages of the book you missed isn't going to change the ending. No matter how many times you read the other half of the book, the outcome will remain the same. All you are doing is replaying your turmoil and pain.

When you read a novel you don't know how it's going to end. Luckily for you in this case you get to choose your ending. You just need to accept that you have reached the end of your novel, if you don't, the story will continue and there's a chance the ending will be worse.

All you need to know is that they had a different story to you. The story they had may not have been the romantic novel you were writing. There are cases where at the beginning you may have started on the same page but the more the book was written, the more different your stories became. There are others of you that will need to accept you were never even on the same page, to begin with. You both started the book for different reasons. They may not even understand their own reasons but this isn't your concern.

Your job is not to understand them better, leave that to them and their therapist to work out. You need to work out your reasons and make peace with them. Your attention needs to be adjusted to focus solely on you. There's a high chance that you had a part to play in your own misfortune, you don't need to take on anyone else's burdens. Their story is irrelevant and knowing their story won't change the outcome. Be honest with yourself about whether your need for closure is you trying to keep that book open?

Are you trying to find out if there are any more pages you can add to the story, just so there is more to read? Do you generally think the answers to your questions will help you close this book? A book that actually you could close right now. The answers to why it didn't work are on your side of the story too. Sometimes after a breakup, we begin searching for reasons to believe in the person again. A last attempt to gain closure is our brain's way of trying to affirm a story that we once thought was true.

Psychologically it's difficult for our brain to comprehend that there are two versions of the story. Our brain wants to believe that only one version of the story is true. What we're experiencing at this time is cognitive dissonance. This is when two beliefs or behaviours about the same subject are so contradictory it makes your brain uncomfortable. Your brain then searches for a way to resolve these two conflicting ideologies. The idea of closure in this sense is your brain searching for a resolution. You convince yourself that if you speak to your ex one more time about everything you'll have both sides of the story. Then ultimately be able to choose one story over the other. This doesn't work though, because you will only hear what you want to hear.

For example

Cognitive thought 1: Your brain believes Ashley is your hero, the best thing that ever happened to you and you will love each other forever.

Thought 2: Ashley sees no future with you and doesn't want to be with you. Your relationship with Ashley was never going to work.

In this scenario, you want 'Thought 1' to be correct. However, evidence tells you that 'Thought 2' is correct. While you choose to believe in both of these thoughts you will never have closure. Your brain cannot be at peace with dissonance. If you do end up having a conversation for closure, you may end up confusing your brain even more. You will learn new things that strengthen both arguments, thoughts 1 and 2. Rather than giving you one definitive answer.

Perhaps you have told yourself you want to meet up with them to talk and gain closure, say bye and end things amicably. In theory, there is nothing wrong with this, however, there is also very little to gain. Even if it is just a conversation the likelihood is that you haven't truly let go of the relationship. If you had, then a conversation about closure isn't something you would need to have.

If somehow you believe that you were the one in the wrong, you may want to apologise to the person, believing you owe them this at the very least. This may be true but this apology is for your own ego and an apology isn't truly going to help the person. If you were the one in the wrong I would hope that you had apologised before the point that you would need closure. Sometimes you have to settle with the fact that not everybody is going to like you. If you're truly sorry you may have to bear the consequence of them not liking you. Gaining their forgiveness is only to help ease your own guilt. You deserve closure and so do they.

You truly have the power to give yourself closure but it's a decision you need to make. Real closure is actually making the decision to close the book. You have to opt-out of feeding into the narrative of this unsuccessful story. This is a story that has already ended so there's no need to add more pages. If you're hoping somewhere down the line you'll get back together, you still need to fully close the book. Accept that if you're truly meant to be together, making the decision to close the book will not stop this from happening. It means your ex will have to work harder to get you back. They'll have to prove to you that you're not opening the same book but starting a brand new book as two brand new people.

If you go back into a relationship as the same person you were before, your book will come to the same end. For you to make it work both of you need to become new people. This takes a lot of work as it requires huge lessons to be learnt on both sides. For you to know you're not walking back into a relationship with the same person you will need to be over them to truly make an objective decision as to whether getting back with them is the right idea. While you are hurt and confused you can't make a decision like this clearly. For now, focus on getting over them, that way it's a win-win situation and you're not continuing to put yourself through further emotional turmoil. The idea of entertaining an ex you're still in love when hoping to get back together is a very unhealthy and potentially toxic one.

Going back to an ex reaffirms Einstein's definition of insanity. Repeating the same thing over and over again and expecting a different result. Deep down you know this, but there is something in you that's afraid to admit that this is true. This is the exact reason you need to be over your ex to know if you should go back to them. Without real clarity you're continuing to add to a story that you know isn't going anywhere.

Try to understand what it is that's holding you to this person and why you're so afraid to give them up. You may have to admit the reason you are holding on to them is simply that you're afraid they will be with someone else and treat them better than you. Fear is not a reason to hold onto a relationship that is no longer working.

Don't convince yourself that you are over him enough to sleep with him one last time either. Having sex with someone you're no longer in a commitment with will only keep you attached to that person. When you break up with them you need to begin the process of moving on. You cannot move on from someone when you keep adding more pages to your story.

Set an objective for yourself regarding that person and stick to it. Write down your objective so it's clear to you what you're trying to achieve. If your objective is to get over them, then you will see that going back to them for a "booty call" is only cheating yourself.

If your objective is to get back with them or gain perspective over your relationship then continuing to sleep with them will not help you do this either. You would only be clouding your judgement and weakening the strength of the relationship you had. Allowing your ex to be even less committed to you and still sleep with you anyway won't give you both the clarity you need.

When it comes to closure there is really nothing more we can do other than learn to accept that the relationship is over. All the other things we do to gain closure are us trying to cushion the blow. By doing this we're only delaying the pain but not getting rid of it.

Dealing with the break up is inevitable and eventually, you will have to face the reality of your situation. The more you engage with your ex the more pain you bring to yourself. You always have the answers to where things went wrong. There's no need to search for more answers from your ex. Another thing we have to learn is just because you feel a certain way about somebody doesn't mean that they have to feel the same way about you.

Don't Twist the Reality

"You've got to learn to leave the table when love's no longer being served."- Nina Simone

When we think we're in love our perspective on reality can become very warped. At times we only see what we want to see. We hold onto the dream that we've sold to ourselves about that relationship. We romanticise the relationship and memories of the good times with that person. We even romanticise our exes personalities choosing only to look at the positive things about them. Forgetting that this amazing guy who bought you a Chanel bag for your birthday is the same guy that called you names and put you through emotional hell jeopardising your mental health.

The scary thing is not realising how unhappy you are living in a toxic relationship. Your unhealthy relationship becomes the norm and so do all the emotions that go along with it. You forget how it feels to be in a state of content. The feeling of waking up and knowing that someone isn't going to ruin your day. Sleeping without feeling anxious and stressed about how your relationship is going.

You don't realise that you've gotten used to treading on eggshells, wording conversations in a certain way so you don't upset your partner. Bottling things up because you're scared to say certain things in case they leave you or it starts an argument. The more time you spent living like this, the more you lost yourself. So much to the point that you couldn't even recognise that's not how you're supposed to feel in a relationship.

Losing yourself is not being true to who you are and how you feel. There are times where you would accept being unhappy just to keep him in your life. All for the sake of the good times you occasionally had whilst being in his presence. This kind of attitude is damaging to your own self-worth. You deserve to be happy and there's no reason you should suffer just to keep someone around you. Even if you lose that person you will be fine. No matter how much you love someone don't put them on a pedestal so high you believe you are nothing without them.

When we put someone on a pedestal like this, we find ourselves in the pattern of romanticism that keeps us going back to our exes and enduring the same issues over and over again. We choose not to see why things went wrong but to cling on to the fact that we still need this person in our life.

We need to know why we're choosing to persevere with someone that doesn't make us happy. It's easy to simply say your working things out. However, when it's only you actively doing the work you have to admit there's a serious problem. Relationships aren't meant to be constant work and struggle. When a real effort isn't there on both sides you have to accept that your relationship isn't going to work.

At times, what you think is love is actually you trying to run away from something within yourself. It could just be that you're clinging onto the future that you've planned with this person. You're so attracted to the plans the two of you had, you don't want to accept failure. Don't get me wrong, sometimes there is the odd occasion where it genuinely is love and your relationship was really as good as you remember.

However, I doubt if that was the case that you would have broken up. Either way, you need to be able to objectively identify a good, healthy relationship for yourself.

Another massive thing that can be romanticised by us is the emotional suffering that we feel. Many of us feel like if the relationship has been hard in some way it makes it special. When it's too easy we feel like we don't deserve it, or that it's not good enough. We think we need to experience all the lows in order to get a happy ending. The longing we have for the person adds to the passion and excitement of them. We're addicted to the rush and anything less than that seems loveless.

In relationships, we're not always aware of how we want to feel. Suffering and love can seem to be part of the same parcel. Many of us have believed that proving you can stick by your man through hard times is all part of how relationships work. By hard times I don't mean things that happen outside of your control. I'm referring to the women that believe one day their partner will stop cheating on them, or stop being verbally/mentally abusive so they can finally get married and live happily ever after. Those that blindly live in misery sacrificing their own happiness just so they can stay in the relationship. By doing this they are simply proving how little they care about themselves.

We need to know what love and healthy relationships are supposed to feel like. Grab your notepad again for an exercise. The aim of the exercise will be to show you how love should feel.

Exercise

Write down a paragraph on what you imagine and expect love to feel like.

Start with the sentence "In this relationship I feel...". When you write this pay particular attention to the following things...

- How the person feels about you and how you know they feel that way about you
- How you feel about them
- How they treat you. Don't say generic things i.e 'he treats me like a queen'. Really think about what that feels like and the kind of things he would do to treat you like a queen.
- How they treat the people you care about and how that makes you feel
- How you feel when you're with them
- How you feel when you're not with them and not just that you miss them but does your mind feel at ease or anxious
- How this person makes you an improved version of yourself

The feelings that you've written down should all be positive and denote a healthy relationship. The big question is if you're honest with yourself, do you/did you feel that with your ex?

It might even be hard for you to believe the kind of relationship you've written down can actually exist. If you struggle with self-esteem it will be even harder for you to believe this would ever exist for you. However, these relationships do exist and can happen for you. As long as you know yourself and what types of behaviour you won't put up with. You have to love yourself enough to not be too scared to say what you want in a relationship. What you've written needs to be your new standard of expectation for your relationships. You should have written something personal to you but it should read similar to this...

"In this relationship, I feel at peace and happy. I know my partner loves me. He is respectful, affectionate and caring. If I need something I can rely on him to help me. There are things I didn't even know I would need or appreciate that he gives me. I can trust him as he makes me feel at ease.

The consistency he shows me lets me know I'm important to him. We are each other's biggest fans, supporting and motivating each other to fulfil our dreams. He encourages all the best parts of me which makes me a nicer person to be around. I can tell him anything without fear of being judged or causing problems between us. I know he loves me because he goes out of his way to make me happy. We have fun together and I love spending time with him. We can be with each other in silence without things feeling weird.

He gets on with my friends and family. Caring about them because I care about them. When we're not together we can't wait to see each other again."

When you look back at your previous relationship in comparison be honest with yourself about whether or not that's what you had. It can be difficult to admit the version of love you were participating in, was not the version you wanted. You may not even want to admit that your relationship was nothing like this.

Subconsciously, you have programmed your brain to believe that the relationship you were in was worthwhile. When it got hard, you believed it would be salvageable. This is an idea you've clung to for so long, in some cases even years it's hard to let go and face the fact that this may not be true. Naturally, we don't want to give up on our dream, admitting that we have failed.

Don't beat yourself up for struggling to come to terms with this. Realise that in actuality the relationship that you wanted isn't what you have. After a breakup, we go through many different stages on our road to healing. It's particularly hard to heal when we're in denial that the relationship is over or we're still bargaining over ways to get it back.

Elisabeth Kübler-Ross conceptualised the 5 stages of grief which can span over into loss of relationships too. These 5 stages are;

- Anger
- Bargaining
- Denial
- Depression
- Acceptance

As we hit the anger stage of our healing process we start to see more clearly. We begin to realise, maybe the relationship wasn't as good as we thought but because our realisation is clouded in anger when the anger fades we often lose the lessons we learnt about the relationship. We revert back to the place of denial or bargaining.

During the bargaining stage, we tell ourselves that there are still ways to make this relationship work. If you feel like this, you should look back at the paragraph you've written about what love should feel like. Then ask yourself if the person you're pining over really provides you with everything you need.

It's a harsh realisation but we have to be honest with ourselves about the situation we're in. It's up to us to put ourselves in relationships that are healthy and make us feel how we want to feel. So many times we get caught up with the idea of someone and how great things could be. Rather than looking at the reality of the person's character we think about what it would be like if that person was to change. This is the epitome of being in love with somebody's potential and not them.

Choose to see your relationship for what it really is/was. Don't judge your relationship on what it **could have been** or **could be**. It's as delusional as getting on an aeroplane and believing it **could** take you to the moon. It's an Aeroplane, so it will take you from country to country, but if you want to go to the moon you're going to need a rocket.

Your relationship didn't make you feel how you needed to feel for you to be happy. If you want to be in a happy relationship you will need a different guy. Yes, your ex could have made you happy if they had acted differently, but unfortunately, that wasn't the reality of your relationship. If you keep clinging onto a false reality you will find it difficult to move on.

Not Letting Past Relationships Cloud Your Judgement

"Turn your wounds into wisdom"
- Oprah Winfrey

When you have been hurt a lot in the past you need to be careful you don't take on a victim mentality. Always take accountability for your choices in life. By not taking accountability for your role in the situation you give the other person too much power.

Often when we're hurt we take the stance that bad things keep happening to us. There's no accountability from us that we're the ones that keep stepping into situations that aren't good for us. A victim mentality is something that a lot of people take on when they're looking at their past relationships. It clouds their outlook on relationships with negativity rather than growth. They feel hard done by about things that have happened in the past.

The problem with this is it means they aren't learning from their previous relationships. The only lessons they are taking with them are the negative ones. If you fail to learn from your relationships you will most likely make the same mistakes again.

You need to look back at your relationships as something you have gone through and overcome. Rather than something you have invested your time into and lost. During any other time in life, when we go through something hard and come out the other side we see it as an achievement to be celebrated. We go to university and celebrate at the end with graduation.

When people get over a long term illness their good health is celebrated. However, with relationships, we tend to look back at the experience as a burden. Something we endured and are scarred from. When it should be something we learnt and grew from. Simply changing our perspective to something positive rather than negative will help us heal.

Yes, we have all been in relationships that have left us hurt but we have to find a way to deal with that pain. Sometimes it feels unfair that we're left struggling to get over something that someone else has done to us. It's particularly hard when you feel like you have given your all in a relationship and it hasn't paid off. It takes a great deal of strength to get over emotional pain. If you manage to do this you're more of a survivor than a victim and should respect yourself as such.

The reality is you have made somebody your world, that hasn't made you theirs. Regardless of this, you have to embrace the pain you went through. Recognise that pain as a moment in your story but understand that it's not your whole story. Don't let it continue to be your narrative.

We all know at least one person that goes from one bad relationship to another then complains that 'all men are trash' and they 'always get treated badly' etc. What they are doing though is placing the blame on others, rather than looking at themselves to see what they can do differently to attract a different kind of man. To make sure they are drawn to men that will treat them well. Instead, these statements are signifiers of a person giving up. If they don't believe there is better out there, they won't bother looking for someone who is better than what they've had before.

They have an attitude that expects men to treat them badly.

The Long-term Effect of Negative Relationships

We've all had that one person that makes our pulse race. The person that makes us anxious or even excited at the thought of running into them. This person is usually a great mystery to us. They were the one that we could never fully figure out, or understand why the relationship never worked. They may even be the ex we feel like we gave our all to and got nothing in return. It may be your most recent ex or someone you were never officially with. It's the person that made you question yourself the most because you desperately wanted to make things work with them but for some reason, it didn't, no matter how hard you tried. They are the person, that sadly made you realise life isn't a movie. That just because you like, or even love someone it doesn't mean they feel the same way about you. It's the kind of love that is usually not good for you, so many things happened that prevented you from being together any longer. These are the situations that in time become toxic.

In real life, it's very unlikely that you will end up with this type of person. More to the point you shouldn't even want to. The dynamic is unhealthy and not the foundation you want to build happily ever after on. However small and insignificant this relationship may have been if you have a person in mind right now they had an effect on you. There may even be a few different people that you're thinking of. Without realising it the dynamics of these relationships may have impacted how you feel about yourself until this day. The effect of the relationship will guide how you behave in future relationships. Unless you make a conscious effort to change this narrative in your life.

It's not just negatively that relationships will have an effect on how you behave. For some people, the effects may have been in a good way, where they realised their worth and vowed never to make the same mistakes again. Others end up repeating the same patterns in search of the piece of themselves that they lost. You may even be one of the lucky people that have never experienced any of this.

For some of us though, there have been many of these people that have entered our lives. The bad news is that we're most likely to blame if this keeps happening as we're the common denominator. Good news is if we managed to get over it once, we can do it again.

Now is the time we can choose to let go of the person that we think has such a hold over us. Regardless of whether or not we last spoke to them yesterday or 3 years ago. We now need to move on from this and rebuild who we are. Creating a new you that wouldn't look twice at this kind of person or relationship in the future.

The worst thing you can do is become comfortable in being the victim. You want to avoid being so used to the victim narrative that you crave the drama in your relationships because it feels familiar. The mindset that bad relationships continuously happen to you is not going to move you forward.

It's time to look inward and understand why you have placed yourself in relationships time and time again that weren't good for you. Identify why you've made particular choices that have led you to the outcomes you have experienced. The whole point is for us to know which parts of us we should continue to nurture and understand and what we need to change.

Relationships in any capacity whether serious or just a fling can be emotionally draining. If you were in a relationship where you were constantly being hurt, manipulated, cheated on or lied to, you most likely lived in a state of constant anxiety. Without even realising it your mental state was being traumatised. Once we have learnt to accept the past and change our way of looking at our previous relationships. There might still be emotional wounds that we haven't healed from.

PTSD or Post Traumatic Stress Disorder is usually linked to large traumatic events such as being involved in a war, car accidents or assaults. It seems trivial to compare breakups with such large life events. However, if your brain has no reference for comparison, then turmoil of any kind is trauma. If something monumental has happened in your life that wasn't a pleasant experience, psychologically you may have trouble dealing with it. The process of your brain trying to deal with the emotional trauma will manifest in different ways. This can be through nightmares, flashbacks and reliving the emotions you had then, over and over again.

These symptoms are some of the symptoms present with PTSD. Rather than PTSD though, this is more Post Traumatic Relationship Stress Disorder (PTRSD). This is most likely to be present if you're leaving a relationship where you were abused. The issue with this is that certain things may trigger you back into a depressed state. This is normal, so avoid being hard on yourself if you have a dream about your ex or see something that reminds you of how he used to make you feel and it makes you sad.

Dreams about your ex may have you thinking you're not over it or even that it's a sign that you should get back together with them. It's none of these things. It's simply that your ex is in the back of your subconscious which is normal because they were someone of significance to you. For some reason, your subconscious has been triggered to remember them. It could be as innocent as you drove past where the two of you had your first kiss, or a song made you remember how you felt about them and now these feelings are coming out in your dreams.

With one negative thought about the relationship, a good day can turn bad very quickly. Everyone has bad days, but you have to know that one bad thought doesn't undo all the work you have done to get over it. Believe that if you let this moment pass then you can go back to the strength you found before. Don't let one negative thought become a doorway for 10 more negative thoughts to attack you. Here's a little technique for dealing with moments like this.

1. Acknowledge how you're feeling.
2. Remind yourself that it's okay to feel this way and forgive yourself for it
3. Breathe
4. Remember 3 things that made you feel happy recently (no matter how small - even if it's something that just brought you a small smile)

The emotions you felt when you were with that person may resurface from time to time. This doesn't mean that the progress you made no longer matters. You went through something that was of significance to you. It's human that you would think about it from time to time but don't let it define you. Sometimes it can even make you feel angry with yourself as you remember things in the relationship that you put up with. This where self-forgiveness plays an important part in letting go.

When moving into a new relationship you have to make sure you've dealt with these emotions and remember what you have learnt. Without dealing with things you will carry this baggage with you and it will negatively impact your new relationship. Admit to yourself what your wounds are so you can heal from them.

Exercise

Let's do some self-reflection, ask yourself what it is that you're doing to avoid being a victim in the future. Write down your answers...

Things to consider...
Have you changed the kind of men you go for?
What are you doing to protect your peace of mind?

Now looking at your past relationships, write down 3 lessons you need to learn from the pain you went through.

Getting Over Toxic Relationships

Toxic relationships are relationships that are really unhealthy. They bring the worst out of you. Your emotions are very intense and explosive. Your worst traits are usually heightened. Angry people become angrier, people with low self-esteem have even less self-esteem than normal. Usually, people around you start to notice that you're not happy or behaving like yourself. These are the types of relationships that break you from the inside. They make you feel less than. It may be that you're always arguing with each other or putting up with more disrespect than you should.

Toxic relationships don't start overnight. You may not even be able to pinpoint the moment when your relationship turned bad. Particularly for toxic relationships, there would have been an accumulation of things. When you look back at it you may be shocked by the number of negative things that went on.

In many circumstances, the dynamics of your relationship were toxic from the beginning. As toxic relationships seem to grow more toxic over time it can be difficult to determine when you should get out of them. The longer you stay in one, the harder it is to leave, because the toxicity becomes normal to you. Many people didn't even realise they were in a toxic relationship until they came out of it.

There are toxic behaviours that other people around you see as a red flag that seem normal to you. Perhaps you identify with depressing songs about relationships because it's the reality of your life. You rush to answer your phone because you can't risk missing his call and creating an argument. You stalk anyone around him on Instagram to see what he's doing. You miss nights out with your friends because you don't want to be accused of doing something you shouldn't be doing. You didn't know how to communicate your feelings to him because you didn't feel comfortable doing so. These are just a few types of toxic behaviours that could have exhibited in your relationship.

You may have unknowingly been the toxic part of your relationship. Doing things to antagonise him and get a reaction because you felt like he was ignoring you. Posting pictures of yourself with other men to make him jealous. Turning off your phone to wind him up so he won't know where you are. These are all toxic behaviours and don't signify a healthy relationship.

The hardest part about toxic relationships is it starts to affect you mentally and can often leave you living with a sense of sadness inside. This sadness sometimes drives you to try harder to make your partner happy. At other times it makes you subdued and you endure the relationship even if it doesn't make you happy. You get used to living with the idea that your partner is doing you a favour by sticking with you.

What we surround ourselves with when we're feeling like this can sometimes allow us to believe these feelings are normal in relationships. We may have friends that are going through similar things. We listen to music that amplifies how we feel normalising our emotions.

When you're dating someone the first sign of them treating you badly can bring up a ton of negative emotions for you. Putting you back in that vulnerable state and clausing you to revert back to the old behaviours that used to help you cope. Something as small as the guy you like, not calling you back when he said he would, can bring you to tears. Putting you in a depressed mood, that makes you not want to talk to anyone. Then when he finally calls you back, you feel elated and cling to him even more. His attention feels like a reward. It's easy to get addicted to this feeling. This is because the dopamine being released in your brain at the time is making you feel rewarded. Dopamine is a feel-good chemical that when it's transmitted it causes you to feel happy. When it's triggered we want to go back for more so we can have that feeling of reward again. We want to keep going back to experience the same pleasure that we felt when he finally called us. The problem is, he only brought us back from the low he made us feel in the first place. Your brain is being awarded dopamine every time he validates you in some way.

We have to be careful of this as it's an addiction that puts the other person in the position of superiority. We can get so used to experiencing these highs and lows in our relationships without realising how unhealthy it is to be addicted to another human being. You become used to this drama and find yourself craving this in your future relationships.

If you have painted yourself as a victim you won't even acknowledge that it's you that likes the chase of the unattainable man. You won't see that you're buying into the drama and repeating the same unhealthy relationship patterns. Allowing your emotions to be up and down constantly.

We really underestimate how addictive this toxic feeling is. For a lot of people, there's something homely about it. It can be normal for us to feel like we have to earn love through trials and tribulations. Experiencing love in a way that is painful seems to make it feel more real. It's almost safer to live in a constant place of hurt than feel the loss of the love that you're holding on to.

The reality is, that there are plenty of people out there that don't have this toxicity in their love lives or in their marriages. These people were most likely hard-wired to walk away from certain behaviours that don't make them feel good. It's an unfamiliar feeling to them that they have no desire to grow accustomed to. If you're the kind of person that doesn't walk away from these behaviours it is because you're comfortable with them. At some point in your life, you were programmed to tolerate feeling like this. We need to identify what these negative feelings are that we've been comfortable with and train ourselves to see them as a red flag.

There is light at the end of the tunnel. It's all about changing your behaviours and re-evaluating things that you think, feel normal. Sitting in a state of anxiety about your relationship shouldn't be normal for you. However, over the years you may have become accustomed to doing this in relationships so see no problem with it. Now you have to rewire your brain into believing that you're not comfortable with negative relationship behaviours. You want to know where you stand with someone. You need the person you're with to actively make his intentions clear and not send mixed signals.

Bear in mind, that it's easier to rewire your brain when you're no longer in a toxic situation. This is because of the perspective you have by not being in the situation, or no longer wanting to be in the situation. The peace you're in shows you how you should be feeling internally all the time.

You need to allow your brain to feel peaceful and content. This is why it's not great to hop from one relationship to the other. You need to allow your brain to remember what peace feels like so you can automatically detect when your inner peace is being disrupted. If someone makes a loud sound in a noisy room people are less likely to notice. If you make a loud noise in a peaceful and tranquil room people are more than likely to notice. It's the same for your state of mind. While your frame of mind is in total chaos any additional chaos you add, will go unnoticed. If your frame of mind is at peace you're more likely to be wary of chaos and avoid it.

Once you come out of this toxic place and live in the content you will be surprised by how you ever enjoyed the roller-coaster of unhealthy relationships. Really take the time to focus on finding peace within yourself. It will help you to be aware of falling into the same negative patterns.

Cheating Says More About Them

Many of us have experienced the displeasure of being cheated on. We've put our trust into somebody only for them to break it. It can be very painful and part of the pain is not understanding why that person fell short of your expectations. The subject of fidelity spans across many different scenarios, not just in the traditional sense we assume it to mean.

Usually, we see cheating as a situation where there's a boyfriend, girlfriend and a "homewrecker". However, infidelity is the presence of betrayal and this can happen in any situation where another person is in the midst of your relationship. This chapter is referring to cheating as when the agreed boundaries of your relationship have been broken. If you have agreed your relationship should consist of only the two of you emotionally and physically but for some reason, there is another person involved, it breaks the agreed boundary.

In your case, it could simply be the guy you liked, made someone else his girlfriend instead of you. It may be that you were cheated on by your boyfriend, or maybe you were the person he cheated with. The pain that we feel in these scenarios are the same. Whatever the scenario is, you were put into a situation where the presence of another woman threatened your self-worth. Being cheated on gives you the realisation that you and this person, were not on the same page and you weren't the only one in the picture.

Along with dealing with the pain and betrayal of being cheated on. You now have to deal with the impact that it had on your sense of self-esteem. In the midst of this kind of betrayal, we really believe that the person that cheated on us was valuable to us. Not only that, but this valuable person in our lives has rejected us.

In order to understand it, we constantly ask ourselves why somebody else was deemed as better than us. Wondering what was so special about them, that somebody would risk losing you. We wonder if we're the problem. Our inner critic kicks in and we start thinking of all the things that could be wrong with us. This is completely damaging to your esteem. It's almost impossible to consider ourselves as worthy when evidence is telling us that we're not. The key thing to remember is, if someone is cheating on you the problem is either with them or the relationship - not you.

We have to make a conscious effort not to internalise the negative feelings we have about ourselves after being cheated on. It happens subconsciously but we forget our worth and focus on the hurt we're feeling. It's when our victim mentality kicks in and our thoughts become depressive rather than helpful. Telling ourselves that these things always happen to us and wondering why none of our exes thought we were good enough to stay faithful to. We compare this to other times we've been treated poorly. Slowly we chip away at our own self-esteem bit by bit. A person's actions are a reflection of them and really have nothing to do with you.

Somebody that's prone to cheat is likely to cheat regardless of how great their partner is. Rather than trying to work out what it is that you did wrong. It is better for you to accept this than to blame yourself.

Firstly, dissecting the reason you have been cheated on is not a good use of your time. Although it's human nature and part of the process of making peace with your feelings, it isn't helpful. To make peace with what has happened it's better that you do this objectively rather than blaming yourself for somebody else's character flaws. The only way to do this objectively is to look at all the factors that could have led this person to cheat on you. This is better than looking at yourself and asking why you're not good enough.

The same way we choose our partners because they reflect us in some way, others are choosing us for the same reason. We pick partners based on what we want to feel. They picked the person they cheated on us with based on how they wanted to feel at the time. Not because the person is better than you.

It could be that they desperately wanted to feel desired by someone new, as it helped settle their insecurities. For some, it's about power. They want to prove that they have power over you, this is especially true for sloppy cheaters that don't try to hide their infidelity. Their need to feel superior means they get off on seeing you panic and fight for your place in their lives. Alternatively, it might just be a character flaw of his that he is prone to cheat.

A person may constantly cheat on their partner because they have a void that they don't know how to fill. Filling a void is a large motivator for a lot of the actions we take. We all have voids, an emptiness that isn't being fulfilled internally. If we don't know ourselves well enough, we will look to other people to fill these voids for us, even whilst being in a relationship. This is especially true when a relationship doesn't fill the void we thought it would fill, or there is a void in the relationship itself.

Relationships are not supposed to be a cure to all of your inner problems. In fact, in many cases relationships can heighten your inner problems even more. The more someone gets to know you and spend time with you the more flaws they see in you and force you to see in yourself also. If you get into a relationship before you're truly ready these problems can be at the detriment to yourself and your relationship. One example of this is, bringing trust issues that you have developed from a previous relationship into your new one. Fear of being cheated on can come out as insecurity that impacts how you treat your partner.

There are lots of different theories about why men cheat. There isn't one answer for all circumstances. The reason why there are so many theories is that there are so many reasons.

The social circle a person is in can have a massive influence on their attitude towards cheating. If their social circle normalises cheating then the chances are they're less likely to value the idea of being faithful to their partner. If cheating is a norm for them and their friends, understanding how damaging it can be isn't something they would consider. They're desensitised to it.

I once asked a guy I knew, why he used to cheat on his girlfriend. His response was very insightful. He told me that he didn't understand why women got so upset about it. He said that women internalised being cheated on thinking it's all about them, but for him, it wasn't. He told me he simply enjoyed having sex with multiple women. Meanwhile, his girlfriend at the time was wondering what she did wrong to make him cheat on her.

His girlfriend blaming herself was a complete waste of her time. She was going over things in her head justifying to herself why he shouldn't have cheated on her because she's done so much for him. What she needed to realise was there is nothing she could have done differently. It was not that she gave too much, or too little it was that the man she was with had no problems with the guilt of cheating.

The mentality he had at the time meant that he didn't see cheating as a reflection of how he felt about her. For him, he could separate sex from his emotions. Cheating for him was about sex and being able to enjoy it with multiple women.

Having sex with multiple women was the lifestyle that he wanted. It didn't matter to him if he was single, or in a relationship. He wasn't ready to give up on the lifestyle he had become accustomed to. He may have really loved his girlfriend at the time but that was completely irrelevant. Love had nothing to do with it as he didn't associate love with sex.

This theory can be applied to a lot of people, not necessarily just men. Some people simply want the benefits of being in a relationship but have no intention of being committed to their partner. They want the best of both worlds. The act of cheating is all about them and their need to fulfil their own desires even if it means forsaking their integrity. It has nothing to do with the women they cheat on or with.

A more interesting question that I should have asked him was what did he gain from sleeping with multiple women? His reason could simply be that he didn't want to miss out on the other women on offer. From a deeper perspective, it might be that he didn't want to form a bond with his partner that was so strong it couldn't be broken by another person. Or more simply his response might just have been he enjoyed it.

Regardless, morally he knew he was in the wrong. Many of these men would not like to be cheated on themselves, but see their own infidelity as something separate. They rarely consider the fact that it shows they're unable to keep a promise and that they have compromised their own values by cheating. This speaks volumes about the type of person they are. If you love yourself, you cannot do things that you feel are morally wrong as it doesn't sit well with you. Loving yourself is all about being happy within and loving the decisions you make. When you lose your values, you lose yourself. As trivial as their reason may seem, them going against their own morals shows a lack of self-love. If this doesn't go against their morals then you know the type of man you're dealing with.

Depending on how people are wired it is not always a moral battle. Culturally people's upbringing can impact their attitudes towards cheating. Most patriarchal cultures value men's happiness over women. Allowances are made for men and women are taught that they have to accept men for how they are. In many cultures, there's almost a free pass that is given to men.

Often there are a 'boys will be boys' mentality that comes with the ideology that men cheat because they desire sex more than women. Along with the idea that it's okay for men to have more sexual partners than women. To a point where it's assumed that it's because of biology that men have this natural urge to spread their seed to as many women as possible, making them more likely to cheat. If a man has grown up believing in this idea. He is less likely to see his cheating behaviour as problematic. He may not be coded to believe that cheating takes any of his love away from his relationship.

Not all men cheat for these reasons there may simply be an issue with the relationship itself. We have to accept that sometimes our relationships aren't working. Not that cheating is the answer, but it can sometimes be the painful result of a failing relationship. When a relationship isn't working it creates a void in the relationship. Unfortunately with some people, the way that they fill that void is by developing a bond with someone else. Them being able to form this bond with someone is not a reflection or even a rejection of you.

Take Shola as an example, she hasn't had sex with her partner Karl in 5 years. This means there is a sexual void in their relationship. Karl then cheats on Shola and has sex with somebody else. Shola has two choices, she can either blame herself and feel worthless because she wasn't able to please him sexually. In which she would be basing her self-worth on how well she can please somebody else. She could then go on to compare herself to the other women and feel inferior in comparison.

Alternatively, she can look at the relationship objectively, recognising that there was a void in their relationship. Acknowledging there was a reason why they hadn't had sex for so long. She would then have to accept that this is what led to the betrayal and that Karl cheating was his response to the void in their relationship. It was how Karl chose to handle the situation. He was unable to fix it or too scared to break up so he made the decision to cheat. It's not because Shola wasn't good enough but because the relationship wasn't.

A better man would have worked on fixing the relationship or leaving. Karl's reluctance to do that says more about him than it does about Shola who stayed faithful. The whole act of cheating in this instance was about him and the relationship. It wasn't personal to Shola or even reflective of his feelings for her.

With all of this in mind, there's no reason you should ever question your self-worth over somebody else's actions.

A Quick Fix to Saving Your Self-esteem

When your relationship ends over the infidelity you convince yourself that if he came back your ego would be restored and your self-esteem would be rebuilt. If you've taken someone back after they cheated on you then you'll know that this is far from the truth. Your ego is not instantly repaired and your self-worth doesn't grow back straight away. In fact, you're often left feeling worse. Think of your self-esteem as a jigsaw puzzle, then when you were cheated on your partner removed some of the pieces. The more we tried to understand why he did it, we began removing more pieces ourselves. Leaving our puzzle with a massive hole.

Subconsciously, we have this theory that the only way to then fill that hole is to get back with the person. It's only when we get back with them we realise the hole is still there, pieces are still missing from our puzzle. They only took a few of the pieces but the hole became bigger because we internalised the pain. Feeling broken, we've taken the person back with the hope that they will bring back the missing pieces and we will feel whole again.

Instead, the hole continues to get bigger as our insecurities have been heightened as we fear that what's ours could be taken away again.

By taking the person back with the hope it will restore your self-worth, what you're actually doing is allowing this person to control your self-worth even more. There are some people that take the person back and then start cheating too as a result of you losing respect for the relationship. What those people are actually doing is still trying to fill the hole they were left with by reclaiming their self-respect. In some way, you may feel like if you get even with him you will hurt less, and that you won't be a fool for still wanting to be with him. However, what would you be trying to achieve by taking such drastic measures to achieve revenge? Ask yourself why you couldn't have just left him instead of cheating back.

We're constantly evolving and should be trying to become better versions of ourselves. Taking someone back after cheating should never be detrimental to you, your integrity and your growth. When you take someone back with the hope of refilling the pieces to your puzzle that they took with them, you're attaching your self-worth to them. The risky part about this is if they leave they will take your self-worth with them too. If he cheats again, even more of your self-esteem will be damaged.

Before you consider taking them back ask yourself what damage it will do to you. Know if you're taking on more than you can handle especially if the person is unlikely to change. Taking them back may not be an act of self-love but you not really caring about yourself in the long run.

She's Not Better Than Me, is She?

A lot of the time the anger and pain felt from cheating is channeled into hate for the other woman. It's easier to hate a stranger than the person you're supposed to be in love with. We humanise the men in these situations trying to understand what he was going through that would have made him choose somebody else over us. Telling ourselves maybe we didn't love him the way he needed us to.

Deep down we feel like even though we hate him for breaking our heart if he chose us over the other woman it would make it easier for us to forgive him. We criminalise the woman for being the person that took what belonged to us.

One of the problems of a cheating partner is while you're trying to understand why it's not working with them, you begin to feel like you're not good enough. Often the situation takes us to a place where we're competing with other women.

Whether it be because they've gotten a new girlfriend so quickly after ending things with you or that they cheated on you, maybe you were even the one they cheated with. It is completely irrelevant, the main issue is that you've been put in a position where you're now comparing yourself to another woman.

Anybody that makes you feel like you have to do this is in the wrong. This is a situation you should never be in, you are valuable. Your self-worth should not need to be questioned. This person doesn't realise how valuable you are if they are willing to replace you, or want to keep you there while you go through mental torture trying to figure out if they are cheating on you.

Comparing yourself to someone else is a dangerous state of mind for your self-worth. It's not healthy and is severely damaging to your state of mind. Whether or not you appear better than them. Either way, by comparing yourself you've put them in the same league as you. We don't need to compare Michael Jordan with Anthony Joshua. They are both great athletes but for different reasons.

How you handle being cheated on is a great way of really finding out where your self-esteem is. Obviously, you shouldn't try getting cheated on just to find out how good you feel about yourself. However, if you find yourself in that situation like this, you should allow the pain to teach you about yourself. For some women, their ego kicks in and they believe the other woman is nowhere near as good as them for whatever reason. In fact, the whole idea that this man would be with someone else over them is completely confusing to these women.

Contrary to women like this, there are those that believe the other woman is better than them in some way. They belittle themselves more and more every time they think about how great the other woman is in comparison. The mere fact that he is with someone else serves as confirmation to them that they're not good enough. It's important for you to know that cheating is not as simple as someone else is being better than you.

It may even make you feel better to believe the other woman isn't as good as you. On the other hand, someone more depressive may begin to idolise that woman. Believing that this woman is better than them in every way. Blaming themselves for the fact he chose somebody else over them. Wondering what they could have done differently to make him happy as she did. Trying to align themselves with how they see that woman so they can feel as good as her. Stalking her social media page to understand what she has that they don't. Comparing yourself in this way will only make you feel worse.

In these kinds of situations, we're never going to be fully at peace. It's not natural for us to relish in the pleasure of something we want being taken by someone else. We deal with it the only way our brain knows how and that's to make sense of the inferiority we now feel. Constantly comparing ourselves to the other person looking for their flaws or ours.

Before we get into why somebody would cheat on you or choose someone else over you. Let's look at the nature of competing with other women and where it comes from. Of course from a feminist point of view, it is wrong to compete with other women for attention.

However, from a primal point of view, it's completely normal. Jealousy is a trait we're pretty much born with. Young children can express it from an early age when they see their parents giving attention to another child. The child often gets jealous and starts climbing onto their parents to mark their territory. They usually aim to be closer to their parents and establish themselves as the priority. There is an instant spark of jealousy and territorialism that is triggered for that child. They immediately want the attention of their parents to be on them instead. Children are also like this with toys too, they don't want another child playing with the toy that's theirs. The concept of sharing is something that's taught to children by adults. We have to learn that it's okay for someone else to have what we have. The idea of giving away something you want to someone else is even less natural.

It's natural for us to hate the idea of someone being with somebody that we believe belongs to us. The fact that this breeds such a negative emotion or reaction from us is normal. It's only natural for us to cling to the person that somebody else wants rather than rolling over and letting another girl have him. It's hard-wired in our DNA to protect what's ours. If we've been cheated on most of us don't want to just give up the guy. The same way we didn't want to give up the attention of our parents or giveaway our toys.

Sadly, by clinging on to that guy you then put yourself in competition with the other woman who also believes that he belongs to her. Both of you have the same goal which is to protect what's yours. Never mind who was there first you're both in the situation now.

It's primal to look after our own interests before the interests of others. In the animal kingdom, the main objectives are to survive and procreate. You even see this with penguins.

Penguins need to choose a mate to procreate with before the season's change when the females have to go on a hunt for food, leaving their offspring with the father. At this time all the penguins begin to mate. The male penguins can take their pick of the female penguins. For females that haven't found a partner yet, there is sheer panic. They will try their hardest to split up any of the other couples. Being aggressive towards other female penguins and trying to split up the couples even whilst they are mating. They are not concerned with how the female penguin would feel if they manage to break up a pair. A female penguin's only concern is with their natural need to procreate. I'm not saying we're exactly like penguins, of course, humans tend to have empathy for others. Instinctively though, we are the same. Our first priority is to take care of ourselves. We don't want to be the only one left alone when everybody else pairs up. This fear can bring out a nasty side of us.

Fear of any kind can bring out a nasty side. Especially if we're competing not to be rejected. Even more so when we're competing to save our ego from being damaged. It's important not to give in to this natural instinct and feel like you have to get one over this other woman. Remember it's not about her. The likelihood is if it wasn't her it would have been someone else. Don't let your hate for her distract you from this very important point.

A guy that is knowingly putting you and another woman in competition with each other is exploiting the fear that we naturally have as women. Especially when he is not clear about which one of you he wants. What we don't realise is actually there is enough love in the world to go around. We don't have to compete with a woman for a man's love. Someone that knows your value would never put you in a position where you need to compete.

Relax in knowing that you're worth more and don't let fear be the reason you take back a cheating partner. We're not penguin's, we don't have to procreate by the end of the season, we will be okay. It's not worth us aggressively attacking women that go for the man we are with or want.

Belittling the other woman is our way of fighting back. We want to understand how somebody could prefer her over you. We begin to be critical of that woman to make ourselves feel better. Experiencing rejection is one thing but having to feel the pain of rejection because of somebody else is even worse. It feels like an injustice. We don't understand why we should be miserable so someone else can be happy. It brings up feelings of inferiority that our brain desperately wants to get rid of. Our ego desperately wants to be fed after rejection like this and belittling the other woman is our only way of doing this. However, this is wasted energy, the time you are spending thinking about her, researching her is time that you should be putting onto yourself so you can rebuild your own self-worth rather than trying to bring somebody else's down with yours.

You may not realise it but you're just hurting yourself further. As you will conclude that either you're better than her, which hurts and confuses you because you don't understand why he would choose to hurt you for her. Or you think she is better than you which hurts you and makes you feel inferior.

Don't focus on the other woman in any way. The thing that we need to realise is no matter how great that person is, or how bad they are, it doesn't take away or add to how amazing you are. Some people love Marmite others hate it. Either way, it doesn't add or take away from the value of Marmite. Those that love it will pay for it, those that don't will not. It's important for you to know that just because another woman has come along it doesn't mean you no longer have any value. Your value is not determined by somebody else's ability to see it.

He may have chosen her simply because he wants something different but you don't need to understand why. We can't understand why some people prefer Chocolate cake over a Victoria Sponge. We just have to accept that not everybody wants the same thing.

Psychologically, the more you compare yourself to her and wonder about her the more you feel a need to win. In most cases just having the guy return to you is considered winning. Everything becomes about proving to yourself that you are not the loser in this situation. This gives him too much power. Whether he wants to be with you or not, the fact the choice was his, meant you were in competition for him. You may believe you have more to fight for than her or more of a reason to stay. He then becomes the prize and you're simply a partaker in this sport.

The more self-worth you have, the more you would resent the fact that you have been put in competition with someone else. Even when you're dating someone, a man that wants to let you know how many other women you're competing with is starting your relationship off with an unhealthy dynamic that ensures he is always the prize.

Your partner's actions shouldn't lead you to think badly of yourself. Your worth is not attached to your relationship. Them choosing someone else doesn't mean the other person is a more valuable woman than you are. His rejection of you for someone else has nothing to do with you.

When you see the person you want to be with, with someone else it's like an emotional bullet to your chest. Especially the thought that they treat her better than they treated you. If you've been with a man and felt like throughout the relationship you were suffering and enduring it, then to see him turn around and worship the ground another girl walks on is understandably painful. Knowing all that you've done for him it would feel like a massive injustice. Naturally, you will wonder if he will be faithful to her. You would want to understand why he would be so good to her and not you.

The difference is, now he is dating somebody different. What he could get away with before with you, no longer works. He's been forced to develop a new strategy. It doesn't mean he's changed so don't feel hard done by. People treat you how you allow them to. It may be as simple as, this new girl requires him to treat her better than you did. This may be a painful pill to swallow but learn from this. His worship of the other girl is none of your concern.

Often the question we ask ourselves is why? Why didn't he want to do this for me? What didn't he see in us that he sees in that girl? The harsh answer to that question is that he didn't have to do it for you. This is because people don't tend to make more of an effort than they have to, to be with somebody.

It may be that you and he were never on the

same page, to begin with, but with this new girl, they are on the same page. Sometimes it comes down to timing. It's a mixture of the right time and how that person wants to feel at that time. The idea that he is a better person now is speculative.

Your focus should be on healing from the split not trying to dissect the quality of his relationship with someone else. You will never know what is going on behind closed doors. His big romantic gestures could mean anything from a cover-up of something to him having learnt his lesson. Unfortunately, it could also mean he's head over heels in love with somebody else. Knowing the truth is not going to help you whatever it might be. Focusing on it won't give you the answer or make you feel better.

The fear of someone that we were with being happier with somebody else can have us clinging onto the wrong person for too long. You shouldn't try to hold on to somebody who treated you badly simply because you're scared that person will treat someone else better. Life isn't fair and we have no choice but to accept that.

People don't belong to us. They are free to fall in love with whoever they want as painful as it is for us. By holding onto them or trying to get them back we don't win. We just invest more of our energy into something negative. We think that we can prove our value over the other woman if we can get him back in some way. The problem is, the dynamic for your relationship has already been set and if you were to get back with him it shows him that you are willing to tolerate his cheating behaviour.

The Only Way to Win is to Get Over It

You need to break the myth that if you took him back he would treat you the way he treats her. Stop believing that being with him will heal your pain. Now, for a few people cheating can highlight areas of their relationship that were broken and they can then put it behind them and move on. Never mentioning it again and with the self-esteem for both parties completely intact. The trust is strong enough to be rebuilt but this takes a lot of work from both parties. You also have to both understand why the cheating occurred and fix the issue so it doesn't happen again.

Be honest with yourself about your reasons for taking your ex back. Know if you are a person that can forget about the betrayal and move on as if it never happened or if it will always make you feel down. You need to be secure enough in yourself to know this relationship won't affect your self-worth. For most of us, it's really difficult to remain confident amidst being cheated on. There's no shame in admitting that you're too fragile to take your ex back.

Many people go back to their ex with the hope

that everything will go back to normal. Then wonder why their relationship isn't improving or bringing them the emotional stimulation they need.

The need to win is what keeps a lot of people going back to their exes after being cheated on. They have to prove to themselves that this relationship was worth it. Prove to their friends that their opinions are wrong and that the relationship will work out. Making sure the other girl knows that in comparison to you she is a nobody. A lot of it doesn't even have anything to do with the guy that cheated. It's a way of regaining control.

Truly winning though is finding the piece of your self-esteem that was lost when he cheated. Being so content within yourself that you no longer care about him being with someone else. Not listening to those voices that tell you to be depressed and that you weren't good enough. There will be no better feeling than the indifference that you feel once you're over someone that hurt you. Plus the look on their face, when they've realised you no longer care about them.

Know Who You Are

Dating with Voids

When we date people, we date with our voids and insecurities. With this in mind, it's not surprising that we would choose partners that fill these voids for us. The outcome of this is that the people we date are a reflection of how we feel about ourselves. In order to move on from our past relationship, we need to begin the process of self-reflection. Knowing where we went wrong in our choice of relationship.

Accountability is king and without it, we get stuck in a never-ending cycle. Accountability gives you the ability to have control over your own life. No more giving yourself over blindly to men that don't know how to treat you. Truly take the time to get to know yourself and your weaknesses. Self-reflection can be a painful process but it's so rewarding. Especially when you gain a new perspective and begin to understand yourself a little bit better.

It's very rare that we try to fix what's wrong with us on our own accord. It's usually when we get to the stage of desperation that we decide to look inwardly and take time to heal. Instead, we distract ourselves with other things. This helps us avoid spending time

with ourselves and asking ourselves how we feel about things that have happened in our lives.

A common thing people do is use another person to distract them from their pain. Taking the time to understand someone else and their needs rather than their own. Trying to fix the places where that person may be broken rather than fixing themselves.

As humans, we're often motivated by things that will make us feel good. We want things around us to reflect our sense of self in some way. The partners you have chosen often reflect your state of mind when you chose them. For example, a woman that feels like she has nothing to offer a man but sex is more likely to date a man that only wants that from her. The mindset you have when you pick your partner is very important, it's why a lot of couples end up outgrowing each other. And it's another reason why you shouldn't get into a relationship when you're vulnerable or hurt. As what you chose when you were in this state of mind is not always good for you.

It's human nature for us to choose partners that remind us of the love we've experienced before. A love that feels familiar to us is far more comfortable. In therapy, you're often asked to look at your relationships with your parents, or lack of. The theory behind this is that your relationship with your parents has taught you how to handle relationships. Your attachment to your parents teaches you how to bond with others and how others should bond with you.

This is why there has been a lot of research

around the concept of "daddy issues" and whether or not they exist. Conceptually a woman with Daddy issues tries to fill the voids given to her by Dad with men. Searching for the male love she's always wanted or is used to. Our fathers set the standard for how we should allow men to treat us. Sometimes the standard that was set can be as transparent as an abusive father = abusive boyfriend.

For other people, it's not as easy to spot. Some fathers haven't set a consistent example to their daughters of how they should be treated. These daughters then may not know what feels right in relationships and spend ages trying to figure it out for themselves. What about you?

Do you know how you want to be treated and which behaviours you're attracted to?

Exercise

Write two lists, one for men you've been attracted to and one about men you haven't been attracted to. On each list write down the common behaviours that you can find with the men you are attracted to and men that you aren't. You will need to look at your past relationships and write down any patterns you notice in the men you have dated or have liked the most.

The list below will give you some ideas about the kind of behaviours that you should write on your list. Only use the ones below if they really resonate with you. Otherwise, think of your own.

Clingy men

Men that are obsessed with me

Unobtainable men

Men that spoil me with money and gifts

Unpredictable men

Womanisers

Bossy and controlling men

Abusive men

Men that lie a lot

Compulsive cheaters

Men I can never get hold of

Responsible men

Attentive

Carefree men

Men that care too much about their image

Stingy

Extremely sexual

Reliable

Untrustworthy

Now you have done that, look at both lists and ask yourself what are the key differences between the men you're avoiding, and the men you date.

This exercise causes you to be self-aware. You need to understand what you are attracted to then we can look at why you are drawn to these unhealthy behaviours.

You may not even think you are attracted to these behaviours but if you keep dating men with these attributes you have to ask yourself why that is. These are attributes that although you may not like them you're not running away from them. Notice if there are any patterns between the behaviours you're drawn to and how your parents have treated you. We tend to normalise the behaviours we have grown up around.

The way we've been treated in the past and the way we see the people around us being treated. How our parents have treated us teaches us has taught us how to manage our feelings.

What feels familiar provides us with a level of comfort that denotes a feeling of love for us. What we don't realise is that our standards are set by these things we have experienced. If you have been taught to expect very little from relationships whilst giving a lot, you will feel comfortable in a relationship with the same dynamic.

Look back at your list and against each of the behavioural patterns you have identified write down what you think may have led to you seeking these behaviours in your partners. See an example below...

Spoiled me with money - My Dad used to buy me things to make up for that fact he didn't spend time with me. Now I date men that spoil me with money but never have time for me.

Men that care too much about their image - I always wanted to be popular and never felt like I was. So I went for men that portrayed the popularity I wanted to see in myself

To do this right you have to be honest with yourself. Really ask yourself why you're drawn to these behaviours. Your explanation for the behaviour you're attracted to should explain what's causing you to be drawn to these qualities in people. Did you go for a man that cares a lot about his image because you wanted to project the image that you look good too?

Does the need for you to portray this image come from the fact that you're so self-conscious about how you come across to the people because you're desperate for the approval of others? If so, you need to understand why you seek others approval so much.

The people that we chose reflect us and how we want to feel about ourselves. Different people carry this out in different ways. We align with people that fill the voids in our lives.

If you don't know what your voids are you won't be wary enough not to use your relationships to fill them. When we enter into a relationship in search of something we attach that void to our partner. The scary thing is if our partner fills that void for us, the idea of losing that person seems unbearable. We cling to them in an unhealthy way. It becomes our partner's job to fill that void for us.

Let's say self-esteem is your void. You're lacking confidence and you meet this man that boosts your self-esteem. He is very good looking so his interest in you makes you feel better about yourself. He then tells you how beautiful you are. If that man, one day turns around and tells you that "you're nothing special". Then he starts picking at everything you do, the clothes you wear, your self-esteem will be even lower than it was before. It is more than likely you will listen to him and want to change his mind about you, rather than seeing him as a disrespectful person that you no longer want in your life.

If you pick a partner that makes you feel better about yourself, purely by them giving you attention. Although it sounds great in theory, it's giving that person too much power. The self-esteem you have should be based on how you feel about yourself not how someone else feels about you. Otherwise, you have an unhealthy dynamic where you need outside validation to feel good. Self-esteem is so important because without it you will look for a partner that you believe increases your self-worth rather than a partner that's good for you.

Pick your partner when you're in a healthy place. If you do that the person is more likely to be a healthier partner for you. Whereas if you choose your partner when you're not feeling good about yourself, then chances are you will end up with someone that accentuates that feeling.

When you were in a relationship or

situationship and the person you were with treated you poorly it's likely to have made your voids even bigger. The longer you stayed enduring this kind of treatment in a relationship reflects how you felt about yourself at the time. Someone that cares about themselves and their wellbeing doesn't stay in situations that make them less secure within themselves. If you endured this type of relationship then for some reason you didn't believe you deserved better. In your heart, you may have known you deserved more, but the voids within you were temporarily being filled by this person making it hard for you to walk away.

Imagine a woman named Nina she's been severely hurt in the past and has been left feeling rejected. She often wonders if she will ever get married or if anyone will ever want to be with her. She hates the fact that she is single and just needs a knight in shining armour to rescue her. She is in search of validation and no longer wants to feel the rejection she is used to feeling.

She wants to feel chosen for once and not rejected. She feels like without being married or having kids she has no purpose in life. All the men that have left her for other women, or cheated on her have lowered her confidence. She desperately wants to feel seen by a man. A man finally choosing her will help her feel validated again. Then she meets Yemi. He seems sweet and really likes her. He tells her everything she wants to hear and finally, she feels seen.

So Nina starts dating him, thinking as long as he doesn't lose interest in her she can get the happy ending she's longing for. It's important to her that he's promising a future with her as without him she will be on her own. She ignores any red flags about him and allows him to treat her how he wants. He's late for dates, that's if he shows up at all. When he speaks about why he was late he is full of apologies and tells her how much he likes her. Plus, he is everything she could want, on paper. He has a good job, an expensive car and is extremely good looking.

She ignores the fact that he only asks to see her at short notice when it's convenient for him. He cancels dates with her at short notice. He never answers her calls and responds to her messages until the next day. Even though he can be extremely flaky, she sees his potential. She sees someone that she can build a future with. She just thinks of him as a work in progress that she needs to invest more time into, to get the man she wants.

In her eyes, they will eventually get married and have kids if she endures the things that don't sit well with her. When she asks him why things aren't progressing, he gives her a story about things not going right in his life. Opening up to her about how damaged and depressed he is. She then begins to see something in him she can fix. She lets even more things slide as she excuses his behaviour and puts it down to his depression.

It's much easier for Nina to then try to help him feel better about his life than for her to realise she needs to take the time to feel better about her own. She believes that once she has cured him of all his problems he will be ready to marry her. In her mind, after that, all of her problems will be solved.

There are so many issues with this scenario. Nina having an expectation of Yemi being the solution to her problem is her first mistake. The lack of confidence she feels from being rejected constantly is the first thing Nina should have worked on. As now, she has pinned all her dreams on Yemi not rejecting her. Nina has put so much pressure on one man to fix her problems. Yemi's job is to validate her and every move he makes now has an impact on her self-esteem. She channels her energy on fixing his issues, rather than fixing her own insecurities. She is interested in the potential he has rather than the reality of their relationship.

Nina entering this situation whilst being so vulnerable has made it harder for her to leave him. It allowed her to accept his poor behaviour because her self-worth was low. She forces herself to believe anything he tells her so she can confirm the narrative she has made up in her head. She would even allow herself to marry him knowing that he has shown her how flaky and therefore unreliable he is. She only looks at the potential of the man she could have, rather than judging the man she does have in front of her.

Exercise

I urge you now to ask yourself what voids you think you have in life. Your voids are any psychological weaknesses you have. Anything that you feel insecure or worried about.

Write them down in your notebook. You should write a minimum of 3 but put down as many as you need to. You may be aware of them enough to know them already.

To help you identify your inner voids, ask yourself the questions below...

When it comes to relationships what is your biggest fear? (every time you answer 'why' expand on the reason, each answer should be longer than the one before.)

- Why?
- Why?
- Why?
- Why?
- Why?

You need to ask yourself why so many times so that you can really understand what your fear is and where it comes from. Once you have identified where your insecurities lie and know what your voids are, ask yourself if the people from your previous relationships fulfilled any of these voids for you.

The point of this is that by knowing your weaknesses, you're better equipped to judge your situations and avoid the negative ones in the future.

When an army is securing grounds for the battle they make sure any risk of intruders being able to infiltrate their camp is eliminated. They ensure that they have evaluated all possible risks and threats. In business, a financial auditor will look at every aspect of a company's books and processes to identify any risks there may be. This will tell them if there's a possibility the company could end up going over budget or losing money. You should be able to identify the risks within your own life in the same way. Evaluate your own processes to make sure you don't invest your time in the wrong things. You should look at these weaknesses again before dating or attaching yourself to someone new. That way you can decipher whether or not you genuinely like this person or just what they represent.

We tend to date people with our weaknesses rather than our strengths. We take our biggest insecurities and the things we fear the most and try to fix them in our relationships. Often we try to distract ourselves from our own weaknesses by focusing on fixing our relationships rather than fixing ourselves.

When we don't put in the work to fix what is wrong with us inside, we will keep making the same mistakes. We don't realise that we are not in a secure enough position to date. We're more vulnerable and it makes it harder for us to feel secure in our relationships. When our self-esteem is low we subconsciously convince ourselves that being treated badly is what we deserve. Unknowingly going after partners that will treat us in this way. Then spending our time and effort trying to fix the issues in the relationship.

Weaponise Your Self-love

Love Yourself First

I've always heard the phrase 'love yourself' and 'self-love'; they've always seemed like flawed terms to me. I thought it was a given that everybody loved themselves. However, I didn't truly understand what it meant. In my head at the time eating a high-calorie Krispy Kreme doughnut at the end of a hard day equated to loving myself. It was irrelevant whether or not, after that, I proceeded to Instagram stalk the fuckboy that had been ignoring me for 3 days. As long I treated myself to that Krispy Kreme I was practising self-love.

Let's get into the theory of self-love. There's so much talk of it in the media and Instagram these days. Love as a whole is a theory that people struggle to understand and explain the meaning of. On Lauryn Hill's album *The Miseducation of Lauryn Hill* there are a group of kids talking about what they believe love is. It's interesting because they all had different theories.

Hate, on the other hand, seems to be a concept everyone knows how to grasp. There aren't a lot of theories explaining what it means to truly hate someone as it seems pretty self-explanatory. Debates around what hate means seem to be a lot shorter. We often think of love and hate as two opposite ends of the same spectrum. Which is why people say there's a thin line between love and hate. However, the opposite of love can't be something that sits on the same spectrum as it. The opposite of love isn't hate, it's indifference. When you're indifferent to something it means you have no feeling either bad or good towards it.

Firstly let's identify the ways in which people behave indifferently towards themselves. Then we can learn how to avoid doing it. Self-indifference is a little bit harder to see in yourself. It is actually worse than self-hate and harder to change. Changing involves you seeing yourself as a person and treating yourself as number one. It requires a complete mentality and lifestyle shift.

The differences between self-love, hate and indifference are simple to spot when you know-how. Once you are able to see it. You will be able to stop yourself from doing this. Whilst getting ready for a night out the person with self-hate looks in the mirror and says 'I look fat' or 'I hate my hair'. The person who is self-indifferent barely looks in the mirror, if they do, they have no opinion good or bad. They don't care how good they look or how bad. They believe nobody will look at them anyway so it doesn't matter. A person with self-love looks in the mirror and says 'I look good' or they do not leave the house until they 'look good'. They do this without going through the negative self-hating talk first.

Which one do you identify with the most?

Exercise

Grab a pen and paper. Firstly I want you to give yourself a rating out of 10.

Answer honestly it's not worth lying to yourself and you don't have to share this with anyone.

Underneath write 5 reasons explaining why you have given yourself this score.

Don't continue reading until you've done this.

Done it?

Okay good, we'll come back to your answers shortly. Your rating is centered more around self-worth than self-love. You have to believe in your own self-worth before you can even contemplate the idea of loving yourself. If you haven't given yourself a score of 10 have a think of the reasons why. What do you think you could do to become a 10?

Many women equate their self-worth to whether or not they can cook, drive or own their own home. Along with how pretty they think they are or how long their hair is. They list all the things they can "bring to the table" to prove their value.

Contrary to this, it's important to understand that none of this adds to your self-worth. Look at your list: what kind of things did you write? Look at your answers and see if you justified your mark out of 10 by how many things you can do that make you "the perfect woman/housewife". Did you put things about cooking, cleaning, baking and looking after your children?

Perhaps you attributed your worth to the material things you own or what you've achieved. Whilst achievements are great and they fill you with pride. It's very dangerous to attach your worth to things like this. It can allow failure to make you depressed. As you would have to re-evaluate your worth every time your business idea failed or you got a bad grade "what would you be worth if you fail at your business idea or don't get the grade you need for your medical degree?".

Did you write down how pretty you are, or score yourself lower because you don't think you're that pretty? I hate to break it to you but if you have rated yourself on any of the above you're attaching your self-worth to the wrong things. When your self-worth is low you subconsciously accept being treated poorly as what you deserve.

Your score should be made up of values and traits that make you the best person you could be. Things that should be on your list are statements such as 'I'm reliable' 'I'm kind-hearted' 'I'm caring'. These are traits that make you the best person you could be. Not how good you are in bed, or how creamy your mac and cheese is. Those things are a bonus, but they shouldn't hold any value to your self-worth. They also shouldn't be what men judge you on or how you judge yourself.

The right man should want to be with you for who you are, not all the things you can do for them. If your self-worth is in those things you will only attract men that want you for those things. While it seems great you're giving them everything they want, it will only sustain your relationship to a certain point.

The man won't see you as anything other than a checklist. You then can't be surprised by how easy it is for those men to start using you or taking you for granted. A lot of women offer all these attributes to men on a plate to show men how good they are. They then wonder why those men leave or don't stay with them when they have given them so much in the relationship.

For example, take Rebecca, she's beautiful and an amazing cook drives a nice car and loves sex. Because of this, she believes she is what every man wants. She dates a guy called Stephen. Stephen comes overeats her food, has sex with her and then tells her he doesn't want to be in a relationship. Rebecca naturally can't understand why. She has given him everything he could ever want, why would he reject her?

It then makes her question her self-worth. In her head, she begins to question why men never want to commit to her. She asks herself what is wrong with her. She believed he should have treated her like a queen because of what she had to offer. Imagine someone that isn't as pretty as Rebecca, they can't cook and or drive would that mean that she should be treated poorly in comparison? The bottom line is none of those factors really matter to Stephen. He wanted to be with someone he felt had other attributes.

These things wouldn't have been a consideration in Stephens mind as to whether or not he should be with her. Those things may make him stick around for longer and waste her time, as he is benefitting from them. However, these are not all that Stephen is looking for in a partner. Ultimately Stephen knows the values he wants in a woman and maybe Rebecca just isn't the one for him. Which is fine because not everybody is supposed to be for you.

We struggle to let people go when we feel like

we have given them the best of ourselves i.e driving them around, cooking for them. Many women fear if they don't do certain things whilst dating, men will walk away from them. Now, when it comes to your self-worth, even bringing up the topic of dating and men's opinions is problematic. Your self-worth should purely be about you, and not the opinions of others. The reason I have brought men and dating into it is that a lot of the time, we subconsciously rate ourselves from a male perspective. We list the attributes we believe they would want us to have.

Look at your list again, when you justified your rating out of 10. Did you write down attributes that you want to have or things that you believe would appeal to men?

In actuality, the score you should have given yourself is a 10. Any other score is a disservice to you. The reason why you should view yourself as a 10 is that at all times you should be the best version of yourself. The best version of you deserves a 10, why shouldn't it? You are not here to compare yourself with anyone else. There will always be somebody you want to compare yourself against but they are not you. You need to be happy with who you are in your own skin. What others think or who they compare you to doesn't matter. There's nothing you can't improve about yourself.

Now, If you don't believe you're the best version of you at the moment, then you need to either be happy with that, which means you should score yourself a 10. Or you do what needs to be done to become a 10 in your own eyes. There is nothing wrong with self-improvement. Time should be taken to focus on becoming a version of you that you're proud of.

Constantly improve yourself to become the person you want to be, whether that means you have to learn a new skill, join the gym or upgrade your wardrobe. Do whatever it takes to make you feel better about yourself. In a way that does not rely on somebody else.

When it comes to self-worth nobody else's opinion matters but your own. As mentioned before you're not a 10 because of the things you can do, the things you've achieved, or how pretty you are. Your self-worth is determined by what you mean to yourself. It's how you view yourself. If you truly see yourself as valuable there are behaviours you won't accept from men. When you truly accept that you are a 10 if a man treats you as less than that you will spot it quickly.

People say we teach people how to treat us. While this is true some people are going to be disrespectful towards you regardless. The difference is that someone with high self-worth would remove a disrespectful person from their life very quickly. They would surround themselves with people that make them feel good. Everyone around them knows the way this person needs to be treated and does so accordingly. Holding yourself as a 10/10 is a lot of responsibility. It means you have to make others accountable for treating you to the value that you have assigned yourself.

<u>Improving Yourself</u>

Exercise

Take the time to do this and do it properly. Let's start by visualising what it's like to see yourself as a 10/10. Think about what would be different about you. Do you dress the same or take more pride in your appearance? Are you living a healthier lifestyle? Get your notebook and write down how it feels to live as a 10/10.

Begin with the following statement "Now that I know I'm a 10/10, my life has changed because..." then finish the statement with your vision.

In business when a company rebrands themselves there are a few things they look at. When rebranding ourselves we should do the same. The first thing which is super important is developing your purpose. This is personal to you so you don't have to make it about others. Discovering your purpose is just so you understand what you want to achieve.

For example, Nike's mission statement aka brand purpose is to "bring inspiration and innovation to every athlete in the world". This is great, for a sports fashion brand as their purpose has to relate to other people. Yours will need to be different if Nike was a person their purpose would be something like "Become the best athlete I can be". The statement now has direction and anyone that encounters this person will be able to understand what is important to them. The thing they are most passionate about has been included. I challenge you to think of what your own purpose is for the next three years then write it down.

Your purpose shouldn't be something that involves other people or helping others, including your children and family. As women, we sometimes cloud our identity in the roles we take on in life. Part of loving yourself is understanding who you are outside of all the roles you have been given in life.

If your purpose is something along the lines of "To become a woman I am proud of" rather than "To be the perfect role model for my kids" you're on the right track. To make it easier, try to use the words I, myself and me in your statement. Don't make it all about your career, the way you look, or things you want to own either.

The statement should be positive and empowering so instead of it being about improving the way you look it should be about gaining confidence. Rather than it being about things you own, it should be about your ability to acquire nice things that you love.

Take the time to write down your statement in your notebook.

Now, that you have your statement, the second thing businesses do when rebranding is to look at the values of the company. These are the principles by which each company lives by.

Your values should ladder up to your purpose. This is done by starting with one core value and then you develop a statement underpinning this value. Your values should be words that summarise what your purpose means to you.

For example, if your purpose is to 'Become a woman you are proud of,' your values would align with this. The values would be attributes that make you proud. You would have a set of values that make you proud. The first one might be…

Value: *Accomplished*

Statement: *I strive to achieve the goals I set for myself*

Similar to the example above, write down 4 values and statements declaring how you live up to your purpose.

Now you have done this you have an outline for the woman you want to be. The next step is changing your mentality. Firstly start by looking at the categories below and write three negative words you feel in relation to each area. Write as many sentences as you can. Aim to do at least one for each.

- ⬚ Career
- ⬚ Friendship
- ⬚ Relationships
- ⬚ Appearance

Now turn these negative thoughts into positive affirmations. For example, if under relationships you wrote 'unappreciated' ' as something negative that you feel. You should write an affirmation that is opposite to that. An affirmation against this would be "I am appreciated in relationships" or if you wrote 'rejected' you would change the affirmation to "I am good enough to be with".

Whatever emotion is written as a negative, imagine feeling the opposite then write down how you would feel as the affirmation. If there are any other categories you can think of, add them to the list.

Put this list somewhere you can see it every day. Even if it's the notes app on your phone or you can write the affirmations on a piece of paper and stick it to your mirror. You should look at this every day and say them to yourself out loud. This will get you in the habit of being nice to yourself and thinking about yourself in a positive way. We want to combat all of the self-deprecating ways you think about yourself. Over time this will change your negative feelings into positive ones. The idea is that as your mentality shifts you will start to align with these positive feelings rather than being a victim of your own negative thoughts.

Knowing Your Worth and Living Like A 10/10

The act of living like you are a 10/10 boils down to you loving yourself fully. The thing we don't realise is a lot of the time we ask people to be in relationships with us and to love us when we don't even feel that way about ourselves. In fact, we don't realise how much we show others that we're unhappy with who we are and how much we dislike ourselves. It's not very appealing.

People generally only want the best. They want to experience what everybody else wants to experience. That's why we all end up watching the same shows on Netflix and buy the same phone as somebody else. We want to be involved with what is considered to be hot property. We consider something as hot property based on the value society has placed on it. We can't expect to place very little, to no value on ourselves and think people will still want us.

That's why it's so important not to enter relationships without loving yourself. If you do, you immediately put yourself at a disadvantage.

The very first part of self-love is actually liking yourself and who you are. There might be things you have done in the past that you're not proud of and things you're even ashamed to tell other people. Maybe it's things you've done or the treatment you've accepted in past relationships. At times, we can be our own worst enemies and we find it hard to forgive ourselves for our mistakes.

In life, you have to cherish your lessons and your growth. If you have done something in the past and you're not proud of it now, it just shows how much you've grown. The person you are now doesn't have to take on the punishment for the person you were then, even if it was only yesterday. Forgive yourself, don't make the mistake again and move forward. Otherwise, mentally you keep yourself in the same place and are likely to continue to make the same mistakes again. It's up to you to make the decision to grow and move on.

Therapy is expensive but life lessons are free. If you've been through something the lesson you learnt should be celebrated and not dangled over your head as punishment. It's important to take time to reflect on the things you've gone through and understand why you made the choices you did.

Part of learning to love yourself is learning to like yourself. Like yourself so much that you become your own best friend. As pathetic as it may sound there is a great benefit to seeing yourself as your own best friend. There shouldn't be anyone else in this world that knows you better than you know yourself as self-awareness is key. This means being able to be completely honest with yourself, especially about your feelings. We often lie to ourselves about how we feel.

Sometimes we even knowingly convince ourselves to do things that don't feel right. This can lead us into emotionally dangerous situations. You as your own best friend will want to take you away from any situation that could hurt you. You should only want you to feel good about yourself.

Most importantly as your own best friend, you will be less critical of yourself. The times that you are critical, it will be more constructive and less mean. For example, you will be able to kindly advise yourself of ways to improve your looks rather than being critical of yourself. The way you look at yourself will be different.

You'll begin to honour aspects of yourself that you don't like. Going from saying things about yourself such as, "my breasts are too small" to, "I'm so lucky I can wear low cut tops without them being too revealing". When you are your own best friend, your perspective on the way you speak about yourself changes. People with high self-esteem feel fulfilled by themselves. They don't need others to validate them or give them purpose.

Spend time on your own doing what you love. When we were children we were our most authentic selves. This is because subconsciously we took the time to do things we loved.

When dating, one of the questions I used to hate most was when they asked me what my interests and hobbies were. This was because I didn't believe I had any. However, that's simply not true and the same will apply for you. You may be lucky enough to already have a hobby that you love and that you're still actively doing. Those of you that don't, need to find one. When you explore your passions it builds your character and begins to fulfil you. Without this, you will start to look for other ways to fill your time, bring you joy and give you fulfilment. When you're unfulfilled by yourself, you could be left vulnerable in your next relationship. You're at risk of making that relationship your passion that you put all your time into. Clinging to it in an unhealthy way.

Trying to find a new hobby can seem difficult as an adult but there aren't any rules to what this has to be. You can find one easily by looking at the things you like. Think about when you're looking for something to watch on TV you will gravitate towards certain types of shows.

Look at which categories those shows fall under and consider how you can become more involved in that specific genre. Even when choosing a book, pay attention to look at the genres you enjoy reading about. The type of pages you follow on Instagram will tell you your interests. Love food, then go to restaurants, tryout different cookery books. These are all signifiers of things you're interested in. The key here is choosing one of them and exploring it in a way that brings you joy.

If you like listening to music go to more festivals

and concerts or learn to play an instrument. If you love fashion, spend time creating fashion mood boards and reading fashion magazines, try and visit exhibitions and go to shows.

When I was younger I had lots of interests that I actively explored. Think back to things you enjoyed as a child and see if there is a way you could do it now. Don't be afraid to invest money in doing things that you are passionate about, even if it's to do a course to find out more on a topic you're interested in. You will only widen your circle and become a better person from this. As you increase your self-worth, realise there's nothing better to invest in than yourself.

Having a hobby is also a great way of finding out how serious someone is about you. If they like you a lot they will go out of their way to take an interest in the things you like to understand you better. Most importantly allocating designated time to your passion will ensure you spend much needed time on yourself.

Exercise

Below you will see a test with statements that you can either rate true or false. It's good to take this test regularly to make sure you're staying on the right track. You can also monitor your improvement as time goes on. The aim is for all of these statements to ring true with you. There is no in-between it's either a true statement or false. Go through the list and note whether each statement is true or false.

- ☐ I no longer give chances to people that continually let me down
- ☐ I know what I am passionate about and actively explore it
- ☐ I have moved away from toxic relationships and only pursue the positive ones in my life
- ☐ I have let go of people that hurt me
- ☐ I don't make myself smaller to make others comfortable
- ☐ I accept that I'm a new person and have forgiven myself for my mistakes
- ☐ I look to myself for validation not those around me
- ☐ I can recognise when someone doesn't have my best interests at heart and stay away from those people
- ☐ I take care of my body and what goes into it
- ☐ I speak about myself in a loving way
- ☐ I take time to nurture my interests
- ☐ I say no to things I don't want to do
- ☐ I'm committed to changing the things about myself I do not like
- ☐ I no longer feel the need to please people other than myself
- ☐ I can stand up for myself

- ☐ I'm honest with myself about how I feel
- ☐ I accept that I will never be perfect but like myself anyway

It's okay if you're still on the fence about some of the statements. There's a lot there, and it's a process. It might take a while to be able to answer 'true' to all of the statements. It's still good to have these statements in the back of your mind. They will help you set boundaries and steer you through life in a way that will help you be kinder to yourself.

Dating Yourself

"We need to do a better job of putting ourselves higher on our own 'to do' list," - Michelle Obama

Whilst temporarily satisfying, eating a Krispy Kreme doughnut is not the way you prove you love yourself. However, the mere act of treating yourself to something you want is a habit that will definitely put you on the right track. Life is busy and at times we can become an afterthought in our own lives. We look to our partners to put us first but rarely do we put ourselves first. As well as taking time to indulge in your hobbies, you learn to become self-indulgent.

Head to your calendar and put in the time for a date with yourself. The reason why you need to add this to your diary is that taking time for yourself is usually the first thing to leave the calendar when you're busy. Whatever time and date you have put in your diary protect it at all costs. Even if it means turning down plans with other people. This is the time that you have set aside to spend on you. Allow for at least 4 hours.

Self-preservation is important, it keeps us sane. At times we need to step back from the world and put energy into ourselves. The purpose of this allocated time is to really spoil yourself. This should be a mixture of soul searching and pampering yourself. In this time slot, you shouldn't use it to do any chores or even any of your hobbies. It should be about relaxing.

If there's a film you've wanted to watch for ages use this timeslot to do that. Don't make it like any other night-in watching a film. Get excited about it, plan what you're going to wear, get your favourite snacks and drinks then turn off your phone.

Alternatively, you might want to use this time to head to a spa for a massage and facial. Take yourself to your favourite restaurant or order food from there. Again, remember to turn off your phone. You could take this time to have a candlelit bath with a new bath bomb.

If you want, spend the time soul searching. Meditate, start a journal or create a vision board. Make sure that when you spend time doing this that your surroundings make you feel comfortable and at ease. That there is minimal chance of you being interrupted.

Light a few candles and create a romantic setting for yourself. You should approach this time the way you would if you were spending it with someone you have been crushing on for a long time. This is all good practice for learning to be fulfilled in your own company. When you love being alone you will only want to spend time with people that make you feel good.

Don't judge yourself for being excited about the time you planned to spend. This time will teach you how to look after yourself and preserve your headspace. Buy yourself a present, could be chocolates, flowers or something that makes you feel special. Often in relationships, we go out of our way to make the other person feel good. We buy them thoughtful gifts or cook them a nice dinner. We need to show ourselves that we're happy to treat ourselves in that way too.

Turning the Attention to Yourself

As we're so used to catering for those around us, we forget to ask ourselves what we want. We concern ourselves with what other people are thinking, doing and feeling about us.

Practice these three things regularly

- Journalling
- Vision boards
- Meditating

Journalling

The purpose of creating a journal is to get to know yourself better. If you've started doing the exercises in this book and have used a specific notebook for it then you've already started your journal. Here are some more things you can add to your journal.

1. Setting goals

Write down your short and long term goals. Try and write at least 5 goals but don't write too many more than that. As you've achieved your goals you can add more. For each goal, you need to write a plan on how you're going to achieve them. This can be anything from a monthly to-do list that helps you get closer to your goal; to a five-step plan. Try to journal on a monthly basis and as you do update your journal on where you are with your plans. Another great way to set a personal goal is to ask yourself a question. This question should be something you want to know or understand about yourself. Then really dig deep to find the answer to that question. It may be that you need to think about that question for a month before you're truly able to answer it. Use your journal to make notes and possible answers. The question you ask yourself can be as simple as "why is my career so important to me?" or "why have I chosen this career?"

2. Prayers and letters
    If your religious praying is something you may do regularly anyway. If you're not religious, prayers are a great way to surround yourself with positive energy and even more so when you write them down. If the idea of praying makes you uncomfortable try writing yourself a letter instead. It means you can go back and

read the letter later or say the same prayer more than once. Your prayers/letters will become little manifestations or wishes. The purpose of these prayers is to ask for blessings. It's like asking for wishes. Put people in your prayers/letters that you want to wish well. Use these prayers/letters to ask for insight and happiness. Spread love to yourself and others. Your journal is a happy place so avoid writing anything negative in them.

3. Gratitude lists
    As you use this journal for positivity, gratitude lists are a great way of taking time out to appreciate what you have. There's no limit to what you can add to this list. You can add anything from spending time with people you love to the roof over your head. It's just nice to take the time out to recognise these things. In the past, I have kept a daily log of things I have received for free to express my gratitude for them. I found that I had a lot to be grateful for at the end of each day. I began to appreciate even the little things like free coffee. Many people do this daily, I encourage you to do the same.

Vision-board

Vision boards can be really fun to make. All you need is a wall, or large canvas if you can't use any of these try an A3 piece of paper. In short, a vision board is a collection of images that reflect your vision for the future. This collage should be made up of images that make you happy. You can have a vision board that reflects either your long term or short term vision.

As time goes on you can add more images to it and take things away. These images should reflect where you would like to see yourself in the future. It should have imagery that represents things you would like to do or achieve, even places you'd like to go.

Anything you would like to experience should be included too. To make your board look for images that you can cut out from magazines or search for them online. When you look at your vision board it should make you feel happy and inspired. The purpose of it is to empower you to achieve the things on it. Everything on it should be about you and what you want to see in your own future.

Both journalling and vision-boarding require time and energy. It's time and energy that you're pouring into yourself rather than somebody else. The goal is to put energy back into yourself rather than other people.

Being selfish has a bad stigma associated with it

but actually, it's completely necessary from time to time. Selfishness reminds you of what you want for your life. You should be creating goals and visions based on what you want rather than trying to base them on somebody else. You will only know what it is that you want by putting time into yourself and asking yourself these questions. You might find that your vision doesn't line up with where you thought you wanted to be or even with the person you wanted to be with.

Meditation

There are many apps and even videos on YouTube that help guide you through meditation. Meditating is a great way to help clear your mind and calm you. It's a great way to calm your anxiety and reduce stress. The practice of meditation requires deep concentrated focus on either your breath, noise or an object. It's really up to you what you choose to focus on but when you're in this state you have to commit to clearing your mind of the usual thoughts that run through your head. Get into the habit of doing this regularly.

Maintaining Your Self-esteem

"Your self-esteem should be protected at all costs"

Get comfortable in your own skin. Loving your flaws isn't going to happen overnight but you need to learn to be happy with what you've got. Putting filters on you and using apps to photoshop away what you really look like is of no benefit to your esteem. Using filters and makeup as a crutch is so dangerous. We need to get used to ourselves and how we look.

Learn to be comfortable with who we are in the flesh. The more we try to cover ourselves with makeup and filters the more we ask the world not to see the real us. We also ask ourselves not to see the real us and to only live the fake creation that we're telling the world to see. There's nothing wrong with wearing makeup to make you look and feel better about yourself in certain moments. As long as you're not trying to paint someone else's face on to yours. No-one is perfect which makes us all perfectly imperfect. Sometimes we focus on one of our features in an unhealthy way. Blaming that feature for us feeling unhappy in life.

Don't get hung up on what you don't like about yourself, focus on the things you love. Love them because they make you different. If you focus on one or two features and blame those features for the reason for why you're not happy with how you look you're being negative and not making the most of what you have. If you then decide you want to get work done to change something about your appearance, that's fine. As long as you're not doing it for the attention or approval of others. Don't do it because your whole self-esteem is attached to you making this change to your physical improvement.

There are many people that change something and are still not happy. Then feel the need to change something else about themselves. You have to fix how you feel internally first before addressing what you don't like externally.

Many people get surgery hoping for all their self-esteem issues to be solved. After this, they're still not happy. This is because rather than looking for a small boost to their appearance they have put all their self-esteem into one thing. The truth is if you've been insecure about something for a long time a quick fix isn't going to heal the psychological damage that was made while you spent years hating yourself. The confidence you wear is the sexiest thing. Until you can master this confidence you will find it hard to be comfortable and happy in your own skin.

Exercise

This exercise is designed to help you build your self-esteem.

Start by writing down 5 things you like about yourself. These should be things that meet at least one of the below criteria;

- Things you admire about yourself
- Things you respect about yourself
- Things you find attractive about yourself

For the next 10 days every day, you need to add another 3 things to this list. One for each of the criteria listed.

Don't Compromise Your Self-love

When we're in love with someone we have to remember we are also important. We are just as important as the person we are in love with. Good healthy love makes you a better person on the inside and out. A toxic negative love does the opposite.

A toxic love will make you fall out of love with yourself. You stop looking after yourself and protecting your mental health. You are no longer a priority in your own life. It's all about pleasing the other person and living for them. There are multiple actions we take that show we're no longer in love with ourselves and are putting somebody over us in an unhealthy way.

It's good for you to be aware of the signs that show you're compromising the love you have for yourself. Knowing these 4 signs will help you avoid doing it in the future.

1. **Compromising your character**
   Our morals and values are key components of our character. Our morals help us determine right from wrong whereas our values are a set of behaviours that mean a lot to us and in a way define who we are. Your morals are a set of principles that you believe are important. They are what drives your character and determine the way you behave.

Deep down, the majority of us want to be good and have others believe that we're good. Only psychopaths and sociopaths get a kick out of hurting others and that's simply because they lack empathy. When you love someone more than you love yourself, you may do things that are at the detriment to your character.

Things that you may not be happy about doing but do it because it makes the other person happy. These things might seem small but either way, it's out of character for you and jeopardises your integrity.

For example, if you were an honest person, that values honesty from others then you find yourself lying to people about your partner or your relationship. It would go against who you are and your morals. It's a clear indicator that the relationship you are in doesn't make you a better person.

2. **Lying to yourself**
    Not being honest with yourself about how you feel in your relationship or about it, is doing yourself a disservice. When we lie to ourselves about how we feel we start to back ourselves into a corner emotionally. We begin to agree to things that we don't want and are unable to make decisions based on our own truth. We go

along with what makes the other person happy. Forgetting that we need to be happy too. This is why it can be easier for our friends to advise us. They see the full picture with a clearer mind. Whilst at times we choose to lie to ourselves about what's real.

We lie to ourselves so that we can see our relationship through tinted glasses, allowing us to live in an unhealthy state of delusion.

3. **Putting up with misery**

At times we choose to live in misery so the other person can be happy. This is a massive signifier of not loving ourselves. It means not only are you not kind to yourself but you allow your relationship not to be either. Your self-worth is at its lowest as you don't believe you deserve better. There are times you may actively choose to be unhappy so that your partner will stay with you.

Accepting less than you know you deserve to please them. Some people even allow their partner to start being abusive towards them. Trying to please them in ways you aren't comfortable with so that they won't leave you. There are many dynamics to this which could be as simple as missing out on hanging out with your friends because your partner has a problem with them or something more complex. This might be knowing you're being cheated on, but turning a blind eye because you're scared of what will happen if you bring it up.

Similarly, it could be agreeing to sexual acts your not comfortable with. In all of these examples, you would be putting the other person's needs above your own. Whilst in relationships there is sometimes a need to do this it should never be at the risk of making you miserable.

4. **Forgetting about yourself**
Sometimes when we meet someone new we get caught up in a whirlwind. We want to spend all the time we can with them. Although that may be okay during the first month or so long term it's not sustainable.

You should still be doing all the things that make you, you. Whether that's catching up with friends and family, reading a book, going to the gym or your regular hobby. Don't just stop doing the things that make you happy because you're in a relationship. Any personal goals you have you should still work to achieve. A good partner will support you to achieve these goals.

Many times people allow their world to revolve around their partner especially when they get married and have kids. While this is fine, you still need to keep something for you.

Otherwise, you'll become too dependent on each other which can create an unhealthy dynamic of codependency. Know how to be happy both in and out of your partner's presence.

Your Ego is Your Shield

The secret weapon for maintaining your self-esteem is none other than your ego. You just need to learn to use it in the right way. Your ego acts as a shield protecting your self-worth. It builds you up and tells you that you're good enough. The purpose of your ego is to make you feel good about yourself however at times it can make you feel worse.

Imagine there being two different sides to your ego. One side, that benefits you, the other can be a slight hindrance. Side A. protects your self-worth and is and is of extreme benefit to you. It believes in your superiority and fights to preserve your self-esteem. This is closely linked to your pride. Side B is the needy part of your ego that doesn't like to be wrong. This is the side that can be a hindrance to you as it doesn't understand rejection. It deludes itself into believing you're always right. Allowing you to cling onto hope in relationships where there is none. Not only that, but it is constantly seeking validation. It's the side of you that decides to post a revealing photo on Instagram when you're feeling low so that all the interest the photo gets can fill you with gratification.

Side B of our ego is most apparent at times when we've been subtly rejected by someone because they refused to meet our standards or give us what we need. We continue to pursue the person to prove this rejection isn't real. For example, Cherelle wants to go on a date with Jonny, her ego is bruised when Jonny tells her he is really busy but will let her know when they can meet up. He is inconsistent when it comes to contacting her and after 3 months of having her number has made no effort to take her on a date. Rachel's ego is offended that Jonny doesn't want to meet up with her. Deep down she feels like he isn't bothered about meeting up with her. She has a nagging feeling that he is not that interested.

The other side of her ego reminds her that she's beautiful and everything he could want, so chooses to believe that he really is too busy to make plans with her and keeps trying with him. This protects her ego from having to admit that she is being rejected. The side of her ego that believes if he really wanted to see her he would make the effort

To use our ego to our advantage we need to listen to it when it's uncomfortable and see this as a warning sign rather than trying to adjust the problem that has caused the damage to our ego. The best way for Cherelle to use her ego would have been to take that nagging feeling she had and use it to protect her from a situation where the guy is not interested.

Another example is if your ego bruised due to someone expressing their displeasure in your appearance. Listen to the side of your ego that wants to protect you. Let this person have their opinion, don't feel like you have to wear even more makeup in a bid to convince them that you're pretty so that your ego can be restored.

When your ego (shield) is damaged the results can be emotionally painful for us. A lot of the time we spend mourning broken relationships is actually us just trying to console our ego. It's not even the pain of the relationship ending that has hurt us. It's the fact that our ego has been bruised. Our ego can't take that someone doesn't want to be with us anymore. It's like when you find out someone you're not even interested in doesn't think you're attractive. On the one hand, you don't care because you don't like them either. On the other hand, you can't believe someone you don't like wouldn't want you.

There are some men out there that our ego sees as the ultimate challenge. These are the men usually referred to as players or fuckboys. Simply because they are often not looking for anything serious with just one woman. It's unlikely that they will commit to a relationship and if they do, are highly likely to cheat. It's in their nature to play games and not to commit. They are the type of men that women looking for something stable should steer well clear of. Unfortunately, they often appeal to us against our better judgement. We tend to idolise these men as they're so unattainable. Imagine what it would mean to our ego if we could tame a man like that.

The ego does like a challenge though and that

challenge is something we need to learn to walk away from. There are times when our ego is protecting us but we choose to ignore it. This protection is the nagging feeling we get known as our intuition.

Something inside us makes us feel a bit uncomfortable with what is going on. We have to learn to listen to this feeling rather than bury it and ignore it. A lot of self-love comes from acknowledging how you really feel and not putting yourself in situations where you have to compromise on your feelings.

Listening to your intuition is a skill. It requires you to be objective and calm. You are following your intuition when you are making decisions with a calm state of mind. To follow your intuition more ask yourself if your decision is rooted in fear, anxiety or panic. If it is then it's not your intuition talking. Listen to the calm rational voice in your head even if it's not telling you what you want to hear.

Setting the Standard

"When someone shows you who they are, believe them the first time" - Maya Angelou

Looking back at your past relationships and how you felt at the time. I'm sure there would have been situations that occurred in your relationship that made you unhappy. These were the things that made you feel like shit. Made it harder for you to sleep at night and felt uneasy with your soul.

Perhaps you got used to living in a state of discomfort. For example, maybe he went missing one night and you couldn't get hold of him. He had a problem with you posting him on social media, or he used to cancel dates last minute. At the time, none of these things felt right to you but you turned a blind eye to the feeling because it was easier to do that than leave him. Take the time to ask yourself if a woman with the highest sense of self-worth would have accepted behaviour like that. Then ask yourself why you accepted it.

You may think simply because you had an argument with him about it, that you didn't accept the behaviour. But unfortunately, if you stayed with him you taught him it was okay to treat you like that. This then set the tone for your relationship. You have to be serious about the standards you set for yourself. If you threaten to leave because of something and then you don't leave, you give off the impression that you don't take yourself seriously.

The concept of walking away from someone over these things seems extreme. Many people can't fathom the idea of walking away from someone if they haven't hit them or cheated on them. It can feel ludicrous to walk away from someone for something so small. We've trained our brains to believe that having standards is crazy. That giving men consequences is us overreacting.

As women, we're almost too scared to walk away from men. Giving them more value than ourselves. If it's us that walk away then we lose them, rather than them losing us. One of the key things you need to learn is how to be comfortable walking away from people that don't value you. It's something you have to train your brain to do as it's imperative if you want to avoid being with people that don't treat you well.

Things we've put up in our past relationships can set the bar for how we believe we should be treated. We see any improvements on the way we have been treated previously, as a positive. Not realising that our past relationship has made the bar for how we should be treated lower than it should have been anyway.

Subconsciously we make comparisons from one bad guy to another. Comparing things as trivial as the fact that the new guy drops you home and your ex never used to. We then assume it means the new guy must be a good guy. This, of course, is not true. It's just that your standards are so low you don't even know what to look for anymore. When dating somebody new you need to look at the character of the person. Along with how they make you feel about yourself.

The standard of how we are treated is set by us. The way we allow ourselves to be treated is a reflection of how we feel about ourselves. How you feel about yourself is evident to other people. If you talk about yourself in a negative way all the time it's a very good indicator to somebody that you're not confident and also insecure.

In the same way, it's easy to spot someone that values themselves because of how they talk about themselves and how they act. Without realising it we give people signals about how we expect to be treated. When they then treat us in that way, our reaction tells them if this is how they should continue to treat us or not. In some cases, this may mean walking away from someone that's not treating us well without giving the person a chance to try and treat you better.

Whilst we may be criticised by some for walking away from something for a reason that doesn't seem that significant. It's your prerogative to walk away when you don't feel valued. Be clear with people about your expectations of them and the consequences of them falling short of these. Someone that knows their self-worth has no problem doing this. They don't want to be treated as less than. When a guy has shown you that he has no interest in treating you the way you desire, then you stay with him any way you're teaching him 4 valuable lessons about yourself.

1.   How much you value him being there
2.   How little you value yourself
3.   What kind of behaviour he can get away with
4.   How to treat you going forward

This is very powerful information for someone to have. If you watch any gangster films, the bad guy always finds a way to control the lead character with the threat of taking away what's the most valuable to them. When you stayed, you showed him that the most valuable thing to you was him. With that information, he knew you would compromise your own self-worth to have him there. The things he could then begin to get away with were endless.

When dating there is going to be trial and error. Part of having standards is knowing what your deal-breakers are. These are the things you will not compromise on. Your deal breakers should be formed from 3 categories. The categories are a useful guide to have as an outline to set your standards about the behaviour you won't tolerate going forward. These are;

1. Abandonment
2. Commitment
3. Abuse

Abandonment

The first category is Abandonment. There are men that trigger our fear of abandonment. These are the men that are non-committal. They say or do things that make you feel like they may not be in a relationship with you for the long term.

At times they allow you to feel alone in your relationship. They may stand you up, turn off their phone or not answer /return your calls for days. Abandonment seems like a strong word but it's the fear that's ignited when these inconsistent traits are present. If you are in a situation where you find yourself with somebody that constantly leaves you feeling abandoned see this as a red flag and leave. Their inconsistency is all you need to understand how they feel about you.

1. You're not their priority

2. They will only be around when it's convenient for them
3. They are not ready to give you what you need for you to be happy

You need to learn to spot this pattern of behaviour in your relationships. If these patterns are visible in your relationship it's a massive red flag.

Abandonment comes in many forms and is largely triggering especially for women with "daddy issues". It's a common trait in non-committal men because their inconsistency also reflects their disregard towards you and your feelings.

In the past we have made excuses for them, believing that they are busy or stressed. Bad at texting and even convinced ourselves that it's just "how they are". If we're honest with ourselves, there is no excuse for it.

A man that likes you, shows you. He will be there for you without you wondering if you can rely on him or not. When you're fearful of abandonment in your relationship it's because **you** have chosen to be with someone you can not rely on. You should only want to build a future with a man that means what he says. Not somebody who gives you false promises. Want to be with someone that knows how to commit to simple plans. Convincing yourself you can build a stable future with a man that often abandons you is a terrible idea. You should want more than that.

Psychologically our brain clings to men like this more because we fear rejection and abandonment. We believe if we can continue to make that man engage with us the rejection won't happen. Unfortunately, it happens regardless of whether you are aware of it.

That man has already rejected the idea of pursuing you in a meaningful way. No matter how long he stays around the fact that he can be inconsistent with you is rejection in itself. Him being in your life is passive he doesn't have to actively chase you, but if you're there he will have you. If he had to be consistent and prove his interest in any way that would be inconvenient to him, he wouldn't bother.

It can be confusing as to how we ended up in a situation with a guy that makes us feel this way. At one point he may have given you a lot of attention and then all of a sudden it stopped. He then began to make promises that he wouldn't fulfil. Constantly leaving you in a state wondering when you will have him to yourself again. There have been times where at the beginning of your relationship he was all over you. It was clear at the time he was actively pursuing you. Then all of a sudden something changed. Struggling to understand what happened, you then spent so much time trying to win back the attention you once had.

Men like this can be like kids at Christmas, they go on about how much they want a new toy. Then after Christmas, once they get it, their interest in it decreases and they want to play with it as much anymore. It doesn't mean that don't won't still play with the toy they begged and pleaded for, it just means it's no longer their sole focus. They like the power of getting something they wanted and then after that everything became a demonstration of this power. Wanting to know that if they were to call you at short notice they could get you to come over, to their house. or if they could get you to buy them something or cook for them.

You should look for consistency in your relationships. Consistency is a measure of a person's interest in you. When a man can prove on a consistent basis that he's into you, you're on to a winner. His contact with you shouldn't be mostly initiated by you. There shouldn't be moments of intensity that then fizzle out to nothing and then go back to being intense. Plans should be made and stuck to and not only made because you have forced them to be made. There may be an occasion where he has to cancel and that's fine but you should be given enough notice and he should plan for things to be rearranged without you having to prompt him. He should make the effort to ensure you have a good time by taking you to places you would like, not just to his house. Remember you only ever see your side of the story. How he treats you is a big indication of what's going on in his side.

If the pattern of contact in your relationship looks anything like waves going up and down you need to respect yourself enough to leave, otherwise you will drown. Going with the flow is not a mode you should feel comfortable with when you know that you want more.

When you're dating, don't be scared to be intentional. You should find out from him what his intentions are. If you have no direction for your relationship it's unlikely to go anywhere. It's your job to decipher if the intentions he has you match with his actions.

Commitment

This refers to the lack of commitment when you're dating someone you see a future with. The level of commitment they have to you is really important. Lack of commitment comes in various forms. It doesn't just mean you're not his girlfriend.

Commitment is defined as "the state or quality of being dedicated to a cause, activity, etc". The keyword being used in the description is 'dedicated', another word for this is 'devoted' which means to be 'very loving or loyal'.

If a man is truly in a state of commitment to you, this is not only shown by him giving you the title of girlfriend or even, wife. His actions show his dedication and devotion to you. A man that gets married one day then sleeps with someone other than his wife the next day, may by title be committed but in reality, he's not dedicated to his marriage the way he promised to be.

In addition to this, commitment doesn't only have to relate to cheating. He could be married to his wife and be completely faithful but not invested in the marriage at all. Spending all his time avoiding going home. Being selfish and not contributing to the marriage emotionally.

A person in a committed relationship is loyal and dedicated to the person they're with. There are many relationships where the couple isn't truly committed to each other. The fact they are boyfriend/girlfriend or husband/wife does not change the state of commitment to each other. Yes, to the world a relationship title does show an outward act of commitment but it can also mean very little when an inward expression hasn't been made. Now, this isn't to say you should be committed to people without the title as titles can be important too. However, commitment should be shown in two ways, one is outward the other is inwards.

The first sign of commitment is showing those around you that you're committed to this person. People will know who you are and what you mean to each other. The other is the sign you show yourself.

Commitment is a personal journey. Only the person that is committed can know how committed they are to something. At times we lie to ourselves about our level of commitment but deep down we know how invested we are.

Imagine we were talking about a hobby, such as training for the marathon. Only you would know how committed you were to training for that marathon. You may tell everyone that you're training for the marathon but unless you actually put in the work you're not fully committed to the idea. Nobody else can commit to that marathon for you. It's up to you. The same thing with a diet, nobody can diet for you. If you want to lose weight you have to commit yourself to workout and eating better.

When you're with a man that isn't fully committing to you but tells you how serious he is about you. You can't force him to commit. The same way you can't force someone on a diet not to keep eating unhealthy foods. It's a choice that a person has to make for themselves. Only they can decide how committed they are going to be.

Neither expressing outwardly or inwardly is better than the other. In a relationship, you need both. Don't let someone give you one and not the other. Otherwise, you'll be with someone that's not fully committed to you, knowing that you deserve better than that.

It's time to start looking in the right places to see how committed someone is to you. Big romantic gestures are not a sign of commitment. Just because someone decorates the room with Roses on valentine's day or buys you an expensive gift it doesn't mean that he is committed to you. Whilst these things are romantic and beautiful. Never use these things as his defence to justify how committed he is.

Commitment is something that should be present on a daily basis. He cannot be committed on Tuesday and Wednesday then not for the rest of the week. You shouldn't excuse his lack of commitment because he bought you a pair of earrings. You deserve a full-time expression of loyalty and love. Not short inconsistent displays of it.

The red flag is the failure for the man to give you the 2 expressions of commitment. One, outwardly and two, inwardly. If you have a man that is disloyal and unloving, you have a man that is not committed to you. If you have a man that doesn't want to call you his girlfriend you have a man that isn't committed.

His actions show if he is fully committed. Only you will know if he is doing the things that make you feel loved or not. Unfortunately knowing if a man is loyal is to you is hard to decipher unless you've actually caught him being disloyal. If you have caught him being disloyal in any way then you have your answer. You know that he is not fully committed.

Abuse

Abuse comes in so many forms and doesn't usually happen overnight so it's one of the hardest things to walk away from. By the time the abuse starts you can feel like you have too much to lose by walking away.

Abuse can present itself in many different ways. This can be either physical, financial, mental or emotional forms of abuse. Physical abuse is the easiest to identify. This is when somebody physically assaults you. Their goal is often to gain power and control over you. If somebody is physically abusive towards you this has to have a complete zero-tolerance response. You must leave them. It's not worth staying with them and finding out if things get worse. Don't make excuses for someone that is abusive towards you or find ways to blame yourself.

A man that possesses such violent tendencies and is unable to control his anger needs to work on himself. This is not something you can help him with. There's nothing you can do that will stop him from being like this towards you. Some women truly believe if they never put a foot wrong their abusive boyfriend will have no reason to be angry with them. They are so careful not to do anything that will upset their partner because they are scared. This is not a way to live. It's impossible to never put a foot wrong in your relationship. If your partner is like this the best thing you can do is leave them.

Only when you leave him might realise he has demons he needs to deal with. Staying there to be his punching bag will not help him and it will break you in the process. Domestic violence is so mentally scarring. Anyone that has been through this or is still going through this should seek professional counselling.

Another mentally draining form of abuse that is actually more common is emotional abuse. This can be harder to spot in your relationship as most of it is verbal. This is when the person doesn't physically harm you but says things to put you down. Over time this kind of abuse can damage your self-esteem and confidence. There are many ways emotional abuse can be manifesting in your relationship.

A common trait of emotional abuse is constant criticism. If you're with a man that is constantly telling you everything you have done wrong or are doing wrong, or how you should look and act. The chances are you're in an emotionally abusive relationship. These abusers are manipulative and rely on your insecurities to bring you down. Your partner may make you feel like you're always in the wrong and that everything is your fault. You end up constantly trying to prove yourself to them.

When you're constantly being criticised it's only normal that this will begin to take a toll on you. As time goes on you would be likely to lose confidence and your self-worth will start to diminish. In turn, the person that is doing the abusing is able to put themselves in a position of power. You begin to rely on their approval in order to feel validated. Your self-worth goes out the window and it's no longer about how you see yourself but how **they** see you.

In addition to this verbal form of emotional abuse. The person may use fear tactics to control you. This is where the abuser uses the idea of emotional punishment as a way of holding power over you.

This can be done in the simplest of ways such as if you miss one of the phone calls, they won't answer your calls for the rest of the day. Their aim is to teach you a lesson making sure that you never miss one of their calls again. Without even realising it your behaviour will change as you would find yourself ensuring you never miss their call. These are the subtle ways that people can be emotionally abusive. Other traits are more obvious, for example, the way the person speaks to you. If the person is calling you names and shouting at you often. They are outrightly controlling towards you telling you where you can and can't go, who you should and shouldn't speak to.

Emotional abuse is all about asserting power over the other person by breaking them down. If you feel like you have started dating someone and any of the signs of emotional abuse are present you need to walk away from them. Otherwise, you will be putting your self-esteem at risk and allowing yourself to become somebody's possession.

The other forms of abuse all centre around control. For example, convincing you that you're crazy is considered to be mental abuse. This is commonly known as gaslighting. Gaslighting is a form of manipulation that makes you afraid to speak your mind, you start to blame everything on yourself. It's where the abuser confuses you, making you doubt your own sanity. They will even go as far as telling you that you didn't see something you saw. If you're suspicious of them cheating they may tell you that you're crazy and paranoid. They make you feel like you're in the wrong for not trusting them rather than them admitting to being dishonest. Some men will even go as far as convincing their partner that they are losing their minds. In extreme cases, the abuser will hide things to make their partner second guess their own sanity.

Another form of abuse is financial, this is where the person controls you financially. They may buy you off with certain things or make you do things for money. Either by offering it, or withholding it. An example of this kind of abuse is when the person showers you with gifts then threatens to take them back when you do something they don't like.

These are all really controlling traits that you need to see as red flags. As with all abuse, there are different levels which can make it harder for you to establish whether a line has been crossed. This is why you need to know your boundaries before entering a relationship. If it doesn't feel right to you don't try and justify things in your head. Speak to someone you trust that cares about you and see if what you're experiencing seems normal.

ACA, abandonment, commitment and abuse are three red flags. If they appear in your relationship you need to be very wary. They are all situations where you are being treated as less than your worth. They cause great pain, which only your enemy would want to put you through. Allowing yourself to be in pain is the least caring way you can treat yourself. The more you practice self-love the more you will surround yourself with things that make you feel good.

Bad behaviours don't just develop overnight either. At the start of a relationship, there will be signs that will determine if you should continue dating this person. If they do any of the things mentioned early on, walking away from him will not be absurd. Staying with him will. Even if you have been together for a long time if his actions towards you make you feel down, leaving him, although it may be hard is only you practising respect for yourself.

Respect is important in any relationship and you

should both have it for each other. Where his respect for you slips, the respect you have for yourself needs to be increased. Many times the opposite happens and the respect you have for yourself goes to. Respecting yourself in most cases is removing yourself from the situation. It's sad because there are so many relationships that have these unhealthy traits. We need to do better than this and stop normalising toxic behaviours in relationships.

Exercise

Under each of the categories for **ACA** (abandonment, commitment, abuse) write down a minimum of one rule that will be a deal-breaker for you. You can write more than one rule for each if any of these categories specifically resonate with you. The more rules you write the better.

These rules are valuable to have and should help you have standards and set red flags. Add to your rules as often as you like. Try to draw on experiences of those around you to help you create more. Think back to your previous relationships and things you didn't like as they should be used to form your rules too. See example below...

Abandonment

Rule 1 - I will not date people that cancel dates with me last minute

Rule 2 - I do not date men that purposely ignore my messages on WhatsApp

Commitment

Rule 1 - I will not date men that try to keep the status of our relationship a secret

Rule 2 - I will not continue to date a man that has been dishonest

Abuse

Rule 1 - I will never stay with a man that has hit or pushed me

Rule 2 - I do not date men that say things to put me down

Now you have set these rules, the next step is living by them. Any compromise to these boundaries will result in you jeopardising the progress you have made. These rules show what it is that you really want. The rules lay out for you how you expect to be treated. It's important that the men you allow in your life follow these. Keep these to yourself there's no need for you to actually communicate them to the people you are dating just keep the expectation in your head and hold people to this standard.

You will be surprised how much people pick up on your new-found boundaries. If someone isn't happy about your boundaries it's likely that this person prefers you to stay in a position that benefits them.

Know Your Position

Know Where You Stand

Know where you stand when you are in a relationship or trying to enter one. So many people find themselves feeling hurt because they simply don't know where they stand in a relationship. They are unclear on what the other person wants from them in their relationship. They spend their time guessing, filling in the blanks and developing their own theories. This can be dangerous especially if your theories don't match up with the truth.

Not only is it important to know where you stand it's imperative that you know where you **want** to stand. Along with what you will, and won't allow. Once you know this don't deviate from it. Stay true to yourself and what you want. There's no good in finding out you and the person you're dating want different things and then continuing to date them anyway. You wouldn't be gaining anything from that. Yes, it might be fun for the time being but if you know ultimately you're going against what you want, then you're selling yourself short. We all deserve to have the life we want. There's no reason why you should be in a relationship that ultimately isn't giving you what you want.

In this day and age, there are so many different styles of relationships. When Facebook launched they had a relationship status known as *"It's complicated"*. It seemed like a joke at first but many people used it to describe their relationship status. Under the description of *"It's complicated,"* there are many different scenarios that you could be in, from booty call to friend's with benefits, to getting to know each other, and situationships etc. There are so many complicated styles of relationships but it's important that you know which one you're comfortable with if any.

Hope is Your Enemy

"Before the word BUT is the lie after the word BUT is the truth"

When you enter into a relationship no matter how serious, it's important to be on the same page. Always be honest with yourself about what you want in future. You're a confident woman with self-worth so your needs matter and should be met. He's not doing you a favour by being in your life you're both there to compliment each other equally. You need to be confident that your end goal is the same as the person you're dating.

If you have the intention of getting to know them to see if the relationship could become serious. You need to make that clear. You're responsible for managing your time. If you allow him to think you're not intentional about what you put your time into you're giving him no reason to be respectful of it.

We often cling to hope when we're dating. We tend to fall in love with potential and then hold on to the possibility of what it might be. Refusing to look at what it is. We take the tiniest sign as an affirmation that what we're thinking about the relationship is true.

I've heard so many women express how confused they are about a man's feelings for them. From actions as little as "we spoke on the phone for an

149

hour last night and today he hasn't messaged me once", to "we had sex last night and today I haven't heard from him". These girls are so confused because one action contradicts the other.

There's a special skill to understanding whether or not the two of you are both on the same page. Once you have learnt how to identify this, it will help you massively. You'll even start to wonder how you never saw these signs before.

One of the biggest things you need to learn is to listen to what is not being said. You need to realise when he **isn't** telling you he wants to be with you. Don't just listen to the things he tells you and the excuses you get. You need to be able to read between the lines. A long list of excuses is not him saying he wants to be with you. It's him inventing reasons as to why being with you is not what he wants.

There are many times a guy is just trying to let you down gently but instead of listening to what he is telling you, you cling on to hope. If he is not saying to you that his intention of dating you is to take things further. Then understand that's not what he wants. The chances are he is not trying to take things further with you. When you talk about the relationship with him, notice if he gives your relationship direction and purpose.

Another thing to look out for is if he uses open-ended language and is non-committal with his statements. Understand that there's a difference between going with the flow and getting to know each other. If when he speaks to you about your relationship but there is no end purpose you need to use discernment to see what is truly going on. If he says things such as, "let's just go with the flow and see what happens". As beautiful as it sounds, going with the flow is not a direction.

Effectively you're being sold a dream. In no other area of your life would you see this as an acceptable response. If you were getting on a boat to go from Jamaica to Hawaii and the captain said he was just going to go with the flow of the ocean, and not steer the boat to Hawaii, you would run off the boat.

If you got a new job and your employer said that they weren't going to pay you. They want to go with the flow before making your job official, you wouldn't accept the job. You would realise that you're not being offered a real job just the hope of one. You would not be comfortable putting in your hard work and valuable time for something that isn't going to pay off. You would start looking elsewhere for a new job immediately.

When someone doesn't want to be serious with you they will often use excuses as their shield. It allows them to let you down gently, without hurting you. They also get to keep you around but at arm's length. A lot of the time it benefits them because you stick around allowing them to not make any commitments to you. They get to have the best of you without sacrificing anything. They probably see how amazing you are and want to be in your presence, sleep with you and enjoy your company. All of this they get without feeling obliged to give you anything more serious.

To be able to tell if that's the position you're in, pay attention to how he phrases things when you talk about making your relationship more serious. If he talks to you about how unsure he is about committing for whatever reason. Whether it's that he's over his ex, or he wants to find a new job, he's moving house or studying. Take his answer as a **NO**.

If he tells you how amazing you are and then says the word "but" this man is not ready to give you what you are asking for and he knows it. Think about when someone asks you to go somewhere and you don't want to. Instead of saying no, we tend to give multiple excuses to avoid telling them that we just don't want to go. It's the same in this case. The bottom line is the answer is **NO**.

All the excuses are just to soften the blow. Ask yourself if it was you, what would stop you wanting to be with that person. We need to be able to understand the difference between excuses and reasons. Rule of thumb is usually that excuses nearly always land in 2's or 3's just in case one excuse isn't good enough.

Another key thing to understand is that there are no such things as mixed signals. Somebody being affectionate with you one day and not the next is a clear sign. They are not interested in actively pursuing you as a love interest. At times they will flirt with the idea of it but ultimately it's not what they want.

Stop giving men excuses for their behaviour towards you. When you have low self-worth you can become susceptible to uncertainty as a glimmer of hope. Because it's not a no and you haven't faced a definite rejection you want to believe things will work out and the man will change his mind.

Everything you do in life is important including the way you spend your time. Life isn't promised, you could die tomorrow wouldn't you hate for your final story to be about you chasing a relationship with someone that doesn't want to be with you.

In the bible, James Verse 1 Chapter 8 it says "A double-minded man is unstable in all his ways". Whilst the context in the Bible is different, the concept behind this saying is definitely true. If someone expresses they are unsure about you for any reason. It's not worth the loss of your dignity to try to convince them to be sure about you.

A man is double-minded when he can't make a decision about your future. The future and relationship he would be giving you is not a stable one. You have to ask yourself why you would seek out an unstable relationship. An unstable relationship wouldn't be a benefit to you.

People can only be sure about you if you're sure of yourself. Somebody sure of themselves doesn't have to convince people how good they are. You've never heard Rihanna try to convince someone that she's a great singer. She doesn't need to, you either listen to her music or you don't. Either way, she's going to do what she wants, your opinion doesn't impact her confidence. When you adopt this mentality you'll be surprised by the respect that people gain for you. Believe that there is no reason somebody should be unsure about committing to you. Anyone that doesn't want to is missing out.

Refuse to convince people of your greatness simply start believing in your own worth. People will then start treating you with the value that they associate with you. Make the active decision to move towards dating people that want to give you certainty instead of hope.

Does Sex = Friend or Foe?

Let's say you've reached a place where you love yourself but just want a man to fulfil your sexual needs. You may believe that you're able to separate your emotions from sex and even feel empowered by sleeping with a man you have no feelings for. This is true for some women.

Some find it really easy to turn off their emotions when it comes to sex. They're even able to cut off relationships with men before their feelings become too strong. Being a woman like this would require you to have total respect and love for yourself so you're able to accurately assess the situation you're in and know when to remove yourself. It takes a strong and stable woman to be able to handle this kind of relationship, not a hurt, broken one.

We can't simply assume that a woman that has sex with many men has no respect for herself. This concept in itself is rooted in a very dated ideology. Especially considering that this theory doesn't seem to apply to men. The self-worth of promiscuous women is often questioned. Many women would rather continue to sleep with somebody that mistreats them than move on and sleep with other men at the risk of being perceived as promiscuous. Women with casual attitudes to sex may in some ways have more self-worth than those that stay with men that treat them badly. If these women refuse to sleep with men that don't appreciate them and are not afraid to move on to the next person for the sake of keeping their number of sexual partners low that is a good thing. As long as this woman is not using sex as a way to fill one of her voids or heal the areas where she may be broken.

When entering a casual relationship you need to understand the value that you place on sex. The more it means to you the less you should share it. If you had to give a £100k away every time you slept with somebody new you would think a lot harder about who you chose to sleep with. This is because most people understand the value of £100k more than they understand the value of themselves. Unless you're a multi-millionaire and £100k doesn't mean that much to you.

We all place value on different things and it's a lot easier to give away something we don't value than something we do. If a woman doesn't value sex it would be easier for that woman not to lose her self-worth the more people she slept with. The time where this woman would be doing herself a disservice is if she allowed those men to treat her poorly, objectifying her past a level she is comfortable with. Or if she did value sex but kept on having it with people carelessly anyway.

Before taking part in casual sex women need to know if they are trying to fill a void by sleeping with these men. It requires her to be completely honest with herself about whether or not she is using sex to seek validation.

If sex is a way for her to feel desired or pacify her pain from previous rejections. This would be the wrong reason for doing it. The best reason she could have is simply doing it for pleasure. It shouldn't be done with the expectation or hope that the guy will start to see her in a certain way.

To engage in casual sex your level of self-worth needs to be extremely high. Otherwise, it's a risky game that could leave you eventually feeling hollow. You could be left unable to fill the void you were trying to cover and have to live with knowing multiple men were able to take advantage of you during your lowest moments.

The worst thing you can do when seeking casual sex is lying to yourself about the real reason why you want to sleep with someone. Casual sex is not a magic pill that will help you get over someone. It will not stop you feeling hurt by previous lovers and shouldn't be used to make you feel wanted or validated.

When seeing someone casually, it's important to keep an objective mind so you're able to tell when you're being disrespected.

You may not even be considering a casual sex relationship however, it's still important to know where you stand on the subject. That way when a situation occurs that has you questioning your feelings on the topic you already have a clear answer.

Exercise

In your notepad, write down the answers to the questions below...

On a scale of 1-10, what does sex mean to you (10 = it's an intimate and special act 1 = it's just fun and I enjoy it)?

If you scored 5, this doesn't count, pick either 4 or 6 so you're not sitting on the fence.

Look at your score and write down your reasons for this score. This will give you something to look back on.

Now that you have done that answer the following questions...

How do you feel about someone sleeping with people other than you? (write full explanation)

How well do you prefer to know someone that you sleep with? (write full explanation)

If you have been in a casual sex situation, or are still in one, what did you think you would gain from sleeping with this person/people? (write full explanation)

Do you like to feel emotionally connected with the people you are sleeping with? (answer yes or no)

Do you whole-heartedly believe in the answers you have given, or is part of it you trying to rationalise past behaviour? (answer yes or no)

Reflect on your answers to each of the questions. Notice what feelings they bring up for you. See if any of them are conflicting if they are, answer them again. Pay close attention to the value you placed on sex and see if your answers mirror that number.

After looking at this you should know how you really feel about sex. It's so important to know your attitude towards sex along with what you can handle.

Your view on sex has an impact on the type of relationships you go into and how you handle them. If you have stated that you don't like someone you're sleeping with to sleep with other people, then you enter a situation where the guy you're intimate with is sleeping with other women, naturally, this is going to be an issue for you. It could cause you to question your self-worth and that's simply because you are doing something you don't want to do, for the sake of somebody else. In this instance, you're putting his needs before yours and hurting yourself.

These kinds of acts are at odds with the practice of self-love. Making decisions that hurt you emotionally is as ludicrous as putting your hand in a fire.

Before you get into a situation, think about what you are truly comfortable with. Don't settle for less than what you know you want.

Defining Your Relationships

Before knowing how we truly feel about casual sex relationships we sometimes experiment with our feelings. Entering situations that don't sit well with us compromising our values for the sake of getting the guy we want. For some of you, the person you're trying to get over might be somebody you were never actually in a relationship with. This happens when we attach ourselves to someone who isn't officially committed to us.

A situationship is when you start seeing someone and it's almost as if you're boyfriend and girlfriend but you aren't. You may even be their girlfriend but it doesn't make them your boyfriend. You may have acted like you were their girlfriend. They may have even acted like your boyfriend but with no definition for your relationship. You entered a limbo with that person known as a situationship.

Just because you were seeing someone unofficially, it doesn't mean that the feelings weren't there. The worst part is situations like this are hard to get out of as there is no definite end. There are usually so many unresolved feelings and questions that we have as to why it couldn't have become something more.

Many of us do this unknowingly at first. Some people even do it intentionally, as they know they don't want to commit to that person fully. Usually, situationships offer companionship as well as sex but without the restrictions of commitment. It's easy to understand the appeal in them for both parties. However, when one person wants more than the other it can become a bit soul-destroying for that person.

Sex buddies, friends with benefits and booty calls, also fall under the category of situationships. Their all relationships that involve no real commitment. We believe that as long as we know that the relationship is purely sexual then we'll be okay. What we underestimate though is the damage this can do to our self-worth over time. How we begin to internally normalise behaviours that come with being in situationships.

We teach people how to treat us, but we also learn how to be treated, by how people treat us. It's a self-fulfilling prophecy. If our standards of how we need to be treated are low, then when we are treated poorly. We don't notice the signs that this is bad and continue to be treated this way. We can't even recognise as we've never known anything different. That's why when we meet a guy that's overly romantic and spoils us we find it strange. We reject it because the unfamiliarity of it is uncomfortable for us.

When it comes to developing purely sexual arrangements in which we've agreed that the relationship should be purely physical. It's important for us to understand the long term damage it does to our self-respect and how we then go on to allow ourselves to be treated.

There are small patterns of behaviours we then go on to accept whilst in a committed relationship, which is to the detriment of that relationship. One example of this is internalising the pattern of being used as somebody's sexual amusement. This can manifest in different ways. Perhaps you begin to believe it's okay for a guy to have sex with you and then leave straight after simply because that's what a "sex buddy" does.

You're okay if he doesn't call you back or lets you down continuously. You become used to accepting this kind of treatment. Then when you start dating someone else you don't see this behaviour as a red flag. This can then set the tone for your next relationship. When you're in a sexual arrangement, you believe the only purpose of your "sex buddy" is to have sex with you forgetting that they're also supposed to respect you too. You forget to humanise yourself and don't require the respect you deserve. This may not be the experience for everyone but it is important to make sure you don't allow this pattern to become the norm for you.

As you're getting sexual pleasure out of the situation you don't realise that there is actually something wrong with someone seeing your body as a wank bank. You are a person with feelings that need to be considered and should be treated as such.

Some sex buddies will go as far as giving you full transparency over the other people they are sleeping with. Then they expect praise for their honesty. There's a line between being honest and transparent and being disrespectful. Take the time to notice which side of the line you feel like he is treading. Your sexual partner openly telling you that you're not the only person they are sleeping with or dating for the sake of honesty, can completely disregard your feelings. You have to be open and honest if that's how you feel. It may be their passive way of telling you that your position is not safe and your presence in their lives is not enough. Imagine if you were to tell them the same thing. What would you be trying to gain from telling them, other than reinforcing that they don't hold a significant place in your life? Take this time to have an honest conversation about how what they have told you makes you feel. A good person will be understanding and careful of your feelings.

It's different if you're only getting to know someone so you're naturally dating other people but when you do know them, accepting them sleeping with other people can be a burden. A common justification I hear from this is "well we're not official so I have no right to tell him not to sleep with other people". This is complete nonsense. You are entitled to feel how you feel and express those feelings to the person you are sleeping with. You are not a ride in a theme park, people don't get to have a go on you and then sample the other rides and come back whenever they feel like it. Without any regard for your feelings. If you're sleeping with somebody regularly you are sharing something intimate with that person you should feel comfortable enough to express your feelings about not wanting them to share it with anyone else. Despite the fact that having multiple sexual partners at the same time can be a huge health risk. If they want to share it with other people and you're not comfortable with this, they shouldn't get to have sex with you. It would mean you're settling for less than what you want. People that love themselves don't settle for less than they want to please others.

If you have a sexual arrangement with somebody, spoken or unspoken. You have the right to express your feelings to that person. If your feelings are a burden to them, then they don't deserve to sleep with you. If you are one of those people that put a low value on sex it doesn't give someone license to objectify you in any way.

Problems start when you lie to yourself about your intentions for sleeping with someone or go into a situation confused about what you want the relationship to be. You are a person with feelings, so be careful not to set up an arrangement with someone where you have alluded to the other person that your attitude is "use me, then disregard me". Men can pick up on this attitude and treat you accordingly, whether you're in a relationship with them or not. It gives them a license not to view sex with you as meaningful. Which it might be, but your feelings should still be valued.

Your attitude towards sex can often be tied to the purpose and intention of why you're sleeping with that person. Have regular check-in's with yourself and know what you want. When you start dating someone and sleep with that person it may mean the world to you, but to them, it may not mean so much.

You shouldn't sleep with somebody hoping to change the way they view sex either. Understand what your attitude is towards sex but also know what their attitude towards it is too. Knowing this will help manage your expectations.

Some people get a kick out of holding their other women over you and the fact you can't say anything about it. Taking advantage of the fact that you feel like you have no right to complain because your relationship is purely sexual. When you have low self-worth you are likely to repress your feelings out of fear the person might leave. I want you to think about what this pattern of thinking does to your self-esteem in the long term. Think about the long term effects repressing your feelings could have on you. Consider how likely it is that in your next relationship you will let things go that you're uncomfortable with because you have that same fear of abandonment.

When you do get into a relationship, and someone is committed to you, you don't want that person to then see you as a sexual object. Unfortunately, subconsciously you could have become so used to being treated without regard for your feelings you then expect your partner to do the same. Your expectation can be for your partner to treat you the same way your sex buddy did. These relationships are totally different so be careful not to allow those behaviours to influence how you behave or what you expect in a relationship.

Navigating a Situationship

"Why buy the milk when you

get the cow for free"

Situationships can be one of the most unhealthy relationship dynamics you can find yourself in. Depending on how they have started and why you're in one. A situationship is commonly used to describe a relationship with someone when you're not officially in a relationship but act like you are. These are negative when one person wants a relationship and the other doesn't.

A situationship happens when you've moved past the dating stage but the person won't commit to you fully for whatever reason. You may even be asking him why you're not his girlfriend yet and being met with numerous excuses. Even though you're pretty much exclusive with them at this point for some reason this person doesn't want to put an official title on things with you. You are allowing them to put you in a relationship limbo, which can become a very mentally draining place to be. Take time to understand their reasons and avoid believing that it's a reflection of your worth. How you handle this type of relationship is very important.

Relationship limbo can be emotionally draining. Often you'll find yourself having to make excuses as to why you would stay in a situation that is less than what you truly want. We all want people to see our value and understand our worth - it's painful when someone we value doesn't value us. It can be confusing that someone we're ready to be with doesn't feel the same way. Somehow we then find ourselves settling for less than we deserve just to keep that person in our lives.

A situationship places you in a position where you have to wait for the person to commit to you. Giving the other person the upper hand by default, you negate your own importance. Putting the other person on a pedestal. You become about pleasing them and validating them, so they can see the worth in keeping you around. In this dynamic, they are the prize and you have to earn them.

You accidentally place yourself in a situation where they don't have to commit to you to enjoy the benefits of being with you. If that's something you're comfortable with, then that's great but often that's not the case and what you're getting is far less than you desire. Do not lie to yourself about how you feel about this. If you're uncomfortable with it don't do it. You shouldn't convince yourself that you think it's okay because it's what he wants.

When the person you are in a situationship with doesn't choose you or takes too long to choose you, it can affect your self-esteem. To a point that you will often wait for them even more, subconsciously trying to erase the damage that's being done to your esteem. The longer you stay, the more damage it does. The answer in these situations should be black or white. They either want you, or they don't, there are no grey areas. Their excuses mean that ultimately they don't want to be with you. You should never leave the door open, waiting for them to decide whether or not you're worth being official with.

What you're not realising is without these titles in your relationship. You're allowing these men to see you as less than a person. You place yourself as merely an option to them. Despite them telling you that, that's not how things are, their actions speak louder than words.

If you're waiting for someone to choose you to be their partner, you are an option. Doesn't matter which way you cut it. As harsh as that seems, it's actually fine to be an option for a short period of time. As long as it works both ways and you see them as an option too. Be aware of how long you would be willing to sit and wait for someone to choose you. If it pushes you out of your comfort zone then it's too long. Uncomfortably waiting is then no longer a good use of your time. The type of man you should want to be in a relationship with should be one that's intentional about you. If someone is dating you with an intention they will not have you sitting and waiting for them too long. Realise when you're waiting for someone that has no intention to commit to you.

You have to remember that it's okay for you to remove yourself from a situation that isn't serving you and it's better that you do. Doing this does not make you dramatic or impatient. It means you know your worth and if someone else doesn't see it, you don't wait around until they do.

When you have professed that you want more from your relationship and the person you're seeing doesn't want to give it to you, continuing to sleep with that person only compromises your own integrity. You begin selling yourself dreams and actively waiting for them to change their mind, which is unlikely to happen. When you're still sleeping with them it shows them they don't have to give you what you need for them to be in your life.

The person may genuinely not be ready for a relationship and that's completely fine. Not wanting the same thing as you, doesn't make them a bad person.

The action is now on you to realise that you shouldn't want to be with anyone that's not ready for a relationship and remove yourself from the situation.

You deserve better than mediocre. Someone that verbalises that they are unable to commit to you for whatever reason is fundamentally telling you they cannot give you what you deserve or want. Listen to the answer they have given you. Don't twist their answer to fit your ego. Remember the letters SLA.

State

Listen

Act

SLA is the perfect acronym to remember when it comes to navigating yourself out of this situation.

State your intention

You should let the person you're seeing know what you want out of the relationship

Listen to their answer

Too many times we let people wriggle out of giving us answers to what we want to know. We assume how they feel and look for only the positive things they have said. Then we draw our own conclusion from there. Don't do this, really listen to find out if their response matches what you want. If with his answer he is beating around the bush ask direct questions.

Act on this

Now you have your answer, it's time to act on it. If the response you have gotten shows you and the person are not aligned on where your relationship should be going you need to walk away.

Many people have a huge problem with the last point which involves acting on the information they've heard. Often pretending that they are okay settling for what the other person wants. They don't stay true to themselves and twist their own truth to fit with the situation that they are in.

When you tell someone what you want from your relationship, the answer you want to hear from them is that you are both after the same thing. Without any excuses as to why they are unable to give it to you. You don't want a non-committal response with no intention.

If they express to you that their intentions are the same as yours with no excuses then you can continue on the route you're going down. If it has been expressed to you that the person you want to be with is not in the right place for a relationship, remember you're not a ladder for them to climb on until they get to the right place. You don't need to be available to them while they go through whatever process they need to to be in the right place either.

Often women believe that they have to stand by a man while he completes his journey. Thinking this proves their loyalty. All it does though is put their needs above yours. Your focus should always be on you, anyone else in your life is a compliment to you. Although in theory, it's romantic to wait for your person to get themselves together. It should never be at your own detriment.

Realise it's okay to let the relationship go if you can't get what you're asking for. You should have certainty over your position, they should equally be trying to drive your relationship forward as much as you are. If they feel they are not in the right place to give you what you need then once they have reached the place they want to be, they can come and find you. Otherwise, you'll allow them to climb all over you in the process of them reaching this place. By the time they are ready to commit it's unlikely they will choose to be with you because the dynamic of the relationship might not suit their new needs. If they do choose you then you would have created an unbald dynamic in your relationship. Normalising the idea that his feelings are more important than yours. Teaching him that your feelings come second as long as his needs are being met.

Without a full relationship title, you may allow certain behaviours to take place because you aren't sure if you have the place to truly express your feelings. You become scared to speak up on certain things so you can prove to him what a great girlfriend you could be. You should never feel scared to express your feelings. I worry about anyone that doesn't feel like they can express their feelings with their partner. Your partner is supposed to care for you and be understanding about your needs and desires. If you're with someone that has no regards for your feelings this is a problem.

Now Use Your Weapon

By now, you should be armed with the tools you need to love yourself and protect yourself going forwards. Reading this book and completing the exercises you should know yourself better than you did before. Learning to love yourself is a process and it may not be instant for everyone. It's important that you continue to do the exercises and read back on what you have written.

Loving yourself is the main weapon you need to avoid toxic relationships and future heartbreaks. When we continue to go through the same situations we have to make a change within ourselves. It's amazing that you recognised that and have taken steps to become a better you.

People that love themselves are happier and more positive. They aren't victims to their situations and? learn what they need to from every lesson life throws at them. As we constantly evolve we are going to be thrown many lessons. The more love we have for ourselves at the time the easier it will be for us to make our way through this.

Self-love does mean moving away from a lot of the things and habits that we're used to. This is hard to do at first but the more positive you become the easier it is to let go of all the negative things you usually hold on to.

Ultimately you need to have confidence in yourself and be 100% honest with yourself about how you're feeling. No longer being afraid of things that make you question your value. Stop being scared to lose people that aren't willing to treat you the way you need them to.

Nobody deserves to feel like shit all the time, at least of all you. It doesn't matter what has happened in the past, forgive yourself for the person you were then. Stop being your own worst enemy and start treating yourself the way you deserve to be treated. Walk into your new life as the glorious amazing you and those around you will notice. You have worked so hard to find the value in yourself. Don't let anyone take that away from you.

My Sources of Inspiration (AKA Bibliography)

Alain de Botton

Why you will marry the wrong person

https://www.youtube.com/watch?v=-EvvPZFdjyk

5 stages of Grief

https://www.verywellmind.com/five-stages-of-grief-4175361

The Truth by Neil Strauss

How the Attachment Bond Shapes Adult Relationships

https://www.helpguide.org/articles/relationships-communication/attachment-and-adult-relationships.htm

Dopamine

https://www.psychologytoday.com/us/basics/dopamine

40 Signs You've Finally Learned To Love Yourself By Rania Naim

https://thoughtcatalog.com/rania-naim/2016/04/40-sings-youve-finally-learned-to-love-yourself/

Acknowledgements

My forever Councillor and best friend forever Jade for being my support. Many conversations and late nights with you have led to me being able to write so much content on this subject. Before I went to therapy I had you, for free! You have always been there providing support and I love you for it.

Thanks to Taranah my sister for inspiring me and helping me throughout the years. Again the many long late-night conversations and having a sister like you has helped me through. Without supportive people like you, I wouldn't have been inspired to do something like this.

Major thanks to Wale for the continued support and always being willing to read and debate things with me during the development of this book. Can't tell you enough how much I appreciated it, even though I disagree with you on nearly everything.

Special thanks to Finan who is always so excited to hear about my writing and Danielle for constantly being on hand to read whatever I need them to. You have always been so supportive of my writing. Big thanks to Samina who I wrote a lot of this book for. Thanks for reading it and trying the exercises with me.

Special thanks to my younger brother and favourite designer Aaron-Lee for creating the cover for me. For letting me boss you around and change my mind on the design many, many times.

Lastly, there are too many names that I would like to give special mentions but at the time of writing this, most of you don't know this book exists. So thanks to all my friends and everyone in the Chapter 30 Debate Club for the support you have always shown me in your own ways. My amazing family, especially my Mum, Aunty Donnette and brothers. My actual Councillor, Jeraline who was so inspiring. And of course God for the strength, knowledge and perseverance I have been given.

Why *The Weapon* was written...

Turning 30 was a huge mentality shift for me. I started to evaluate my life and finally take accountability for the choices I had made. I made a decision to become the best version of myself that I could be. I got into therapy and started on the journey. I learnt so much about myself and found a new love for me, that I never had before. After therapy, I felt great and decided I wanted to write a book to teach other women how to feel as good as I did. I wanted to write something I wished I had been given five years earlier. *The Weapon* is that book.

Printed in Great Britain
by Amazon